Technology on a Shoestring

A Survival Guide for Educators and Other Professionals

Technology on a Shoestring

A Survival Guide for
Educators and Other Professionals

THANE B. TERRILL

Teachers College, Columbia University
New York and London

Published by Teachers College Press, 1234 Amsterdam Avenue, New York, NY 10027

Library of Congress Cataloging-in-Publication Data

Terrill, Thane B.
    Technology on a shoestring : a survival guide for educators and
  other professionals / Thane B. Terrill.
      p. cm.
    Includes bibliographical references and index.
    ISBN-13: 978-0-8077-4649-3 (pbk. : alk. paper)
    ISBN-10: 0-8077-4649-5 (pbk.)
    1. Educational technology—Planning.   I. Title.
    LB1028.3.T468 2006
    371.33—dc22   2006002470

ISBN-13: 978-0-8077-4649-3   ISBN-10: 0-8077-4649-5

Printed on acid-free paper
Manufactured in the United States of America

13 12 11 10 09 08 07 06   8 7 6 5 4 3 2 1

Contents

Introduction

You got to be very careful if you don't know where you're going,
because you might not get there.

—Yogi Berra

It was not that long ago that overhead projectors and ditto machines were the only forms of high-tech found in a school. Today's educator works within a web of technologies ranging from barcode readers to virtual reality displays. Technology has made education more effective, but not easier. If you are like most educators, you never had the opportunity to take a course related to using technology in schools. In fact many educators never saw more than a typewriter as a student. Yet without training, and in some cases without direct experience, teachers are expected to transform their lesson plans into veritable multimedia extravaganzas.

While *Technology on a Shoestring* is targeted at technical coordinators, computer lab instructors, and librarians, it is useful for anyone who deals with technology within schools. This book will help principals and other decisionmakers to evaluate technology plans and budgets. Even students can benefit from reading some of chapters as preparation for working on an in-school technical support team. In other words: If you're in a school, there is something here for you.

Making technology work in the educational environment is more difficult that it would initially seem to be. There is an understandable assumption that

Figure 1. Mimeograph Machine

1

computer technology in the corporate environment is vastly more complex than the seemingly simpler computer networks found in the typical school. In terms of total complexity, business systems can be very complex and they are often deployed on massive scales. They are also fully tested and well-supported by vendors. Likewise, businesses have the deep pockets required to keep software current, to create prototype systems, to have highly trained technical staffs, and, when all else fails, to bring in top-caliber consultants. But beyond the issue of support is that of design. Most computer hardware and software is designed for the business environment. The educational market, even for those firms with educational divisions, is pretty much an afterthought: Next time you get a new computer purchased on a school account, check to see if they sent a keyboard designed for children or for adults.

Software applications are frequently designed for the adult corporate user, and sometimes adapted for use by children. No one has to label a word processor "for adults"—it's just assumed; but if one is designed for the educational market, it is labeled as such. So, not only are your tools less well supported than they would be for a corporate environment; they are actually designed for corporate use.

The way in which technology entered the school environment is also quite different than for the corporation, which started with expensive mainframe computers and then later moved to personal computers and computer networks. Schools, on the other hand, usually started with one or two personal computers, perhaps in the school's administration office, then they spread to the computer lab, then to classrooms, and then to a unified network. This is a critical difference because, in the school environment, the person who was picked to take care of the computers was often initially picked to take care of just a few computers. As the system grew, the skills required may have exceeded the skills that were originally needed. So, while business networks have gone from highly complex to less complex technologies, school networks have gone from simple to complex. Obviously, it is easier for a mainframe expert to move into networks of PCs than it is for a math teacher to go from running his or her own computer to networks of PCs.

Don't be depressed. Rather, you should have a sense of pride in your accomplishment. This book is not for the corporate user—if that's you, go read one of dozens of books written just for you. This book looks at technology as it really exists in the typical K–12 school environment and presents solutions to common issues.

What Is a Network?

Naturally, any book with the word *network* in it should provide a definition of a network. The standard definition is, a network is an interconnected collection of devices. In most cases this will mean computers, printers, and the wires, switches, hubs, and routers which connect them. Yet the Internet and the internal hardware of a computer are also networks. Sun Microsystems' famous motto, "The network is the computer," is a perfect example of how everything is the same. Only the scale changes.

Any definition of a network that does not include social and nontechnical networks is lacking. Technical networks are in some ways enclosed systems, yet they function within the dynamics of social and other nontechnical networks. For example, an application that shares information on car pooling may be superior to the old-fashioned bulletin board—or it may not. It all depends on scale, complexity, and the organization's culture.

Social networks are important for a variety of reasons. If an organization has a well-established method for sharing certain types of information, a superior technical solution may flounder simply because people are creatures of habit and often prefer routines with which they are comfortable. Furthermore, your new project may have the effect of removing a significant portion of a colleague's job responsibilities. Don't be surprised when your soon-to-be irrelevant colleagues oppose your improvements. It's important to realize that technology is only one issue that you need to consider. Most people who have had great projects die for no apparent reason ran aground on the shoals of undocumented networks.

Recognizing the Impact of Technology

More than one technologist has been taken aback by the stiff resistance of users whom they thought were going to be helped. Because society views technology as an almost universal good, resistance to technology is often cloaked with excuses: "I don't have time to learn," or "It doesn't work for me." A technologist who takes these statements at face value may respond: "You'll have more time once you starting using the computer" or "I'll be happy to show you how it works." The user may be coerced into a training session or two. In these cases, the core problems were really not addressed.

For some staff, technology may be perceived as the first step of phasing out their jobs. Others may fear that they will now be viewed as incompetent after long years of mastering the old system. From earliest times, the teacher was the one with the knowledge and the student was the one in need of knowledge. The teacher was, for all intents and purposes, the oracle of all information. If it did not come out of the teacher's mouth or from a book assigned by the teacher, it was not part of the course. In many countries, the teacher still reads from a book and the students recite it back. The computer is a sea change unlike anything that has happened since the printing press. Now the teacher is competing with other sources of information. The teacher's role has effectively been transformed from that of an oracle to one of a coach. Major change is always scary.

New technologies can be frightening even for the teacher who eagerly wants to use them. Anyone who has stood in front of a class knows that interruptions to the flow of the lesson can be disastrous. It doesn't take much to set things spinning out of control. A computer breaks down and along with it goes that day's lesson plan. A group of students complain that their computer is broken and thus cannot turn in the assignment on time. A third grader accidentally finds a porn site and everyone wants to see. Before the computer, teachers were the "computer" and if they were broken down, they didn't have to worry because they were at home and substitutes were teaching the class. When something bad occurs with technology, teachers may wish they were at home.

The Basic Elements of a Computer Network

The computer is the building brick of the modern computer network. While it is possible to have a network without anything resembling a computer attached, the majority of school networks are built with the intention of servicing and extending the capabilities of its personal computers. The key to understanding a network diagram is to focus on the PC and trace the services that connect to it. Don't get discouraged by computer network diagrams that looks like the innards of a car engine. Overlay enough simple objects and anything will look complex.

Figure 2. The Evolution of Computer Memory

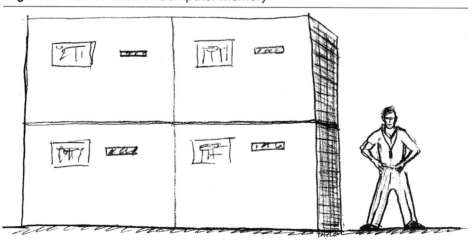

Beside the computer technologist depicted above are four identical 1302 memory banks manufactured in 1965. All four units together offered a capacity of 800 MB. The total price in 2006 dollars would be $10 million. By contrast, the flashdrive dangling from the technologist's neck can hold 1,000 MB at a price of $50.

The first computers were self-contained. Computer operators manually connected wires between different holes on a circuit board in order to give instructions. Keyboards came later. There were no network connections, floppy disk drives, or monitors. Instead of a monitor, the results might be represented by a series of lights on the computer's front panel. Not surprisingly, people looked for better ways. Keyboards and monitors immensely increased the speed with which commands could be entered and the results read. Rather than retype commands every time a program needed to run, computer engineers added paper tapes with holes punched in strategic locations, followed by punch cards, followed by magnet media. Early magnetic storage units could hold less than today's smallest USB storage device.

The first networks of personal computers came into being for two primary reasons—to share expensive equipment and to enable data sharing between users. The first form of networking was called "sneaker net"—people walked from place to place with diskette in hand. The progenitor of the personal computer network was device sharing. When a printer costs thousands of dollars, the solution is to share it between users. In some places this meant handing a diskette with the file to be printed to the user with the printer. Needless to say, that was annoying. So switch boxes that could allow multiple computers to share a printer if they were close by were developed. Mainframes had long had well-established networks, but their paradigms were all based on communicating with a central computer. It was not until the early 1980s that the first network operating systems came to market that could allow PCs to communicate easily between themselves and with peripherals, such as printers and remote storage.

The first PCs were seen by the mainframe computer experts—and they were the only computer experts of that time—as curiosities and toys. Computer experts were exclusively to be found working on large computer mainframes housed in "glass rooms" (so named because the air-conditioned computer centers often had glass walls). These technologists were seen by the users—and by themselves—as high priests of the computer center. The high priest often looked down on the early PCs and did whatever they could to restrict PCs in the office environment. Users rebelled by purchasing PCs under the "furniture budget" and sneaking in their new "furniture." The high priests were not amused, but they could do little because they did not control the "furniture" budget and the PCs were not at that time connected to the company's mainframe.

Eventually PCs were recognized as a legitimate part of the organization's computer operation. K–12 schools did not go through this process because mainframes and the "high priests" who attended to them were either not present or were located in some distant district or regional headquarters. The history of the PC in the corporate environment is important to know because the development of the technology that has come down to the schools was, and continues to be, influenced by the dynamics of the corporate environment.

How Things Communicate

Networking computers is at one level about hardware and at another level about protocols and standards that instruct the systems on how to do their work. Any device on a network needs to answer the following questions:

1. Is there a network?
2. Is the connection working reliably?
3. How are connections to other devices made?
4. How is information sent between devices?
5. How are problems discovered and handled?

Computer scientists describe networks as having "layers." The most common description is the OSI seven-layer model. These layers essentially answer the five questions just listed. In the OSI model, each layer depends on all the ones beneath it to function. The bottom layer is layer 1 and the highest layer is layer 7. Layer 1 is the foundation and layer 7 is the layer to which the computer user has direct access. The OSI seven-layer model is actually very useful to understanding a computer network. Network problems become a lot less mysterious when you know in which area of the model the problem resides. This model applies just as well to a home network comprised of two computers as it does to the Internet's backbone infrastructure. Here is a list of the seven layers and the potential problems associated with each layer.

Figure 3. Seven-Layer Model

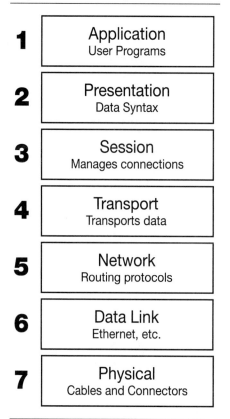

1. **Physical Layer:** This layer is about the physical wire and signals being sent across it. Cut cables and other physical problems are associated with this layer.
2. **Data Link Layer:** The physical layer is monitored and the flow of data between devices is handled. Interference or weak signals are possible problems with this layer.
3. **Network Layer:** This layer essentially puts the address on the data. It can be seen as an envelope for the data. Misconfigured networks are the principal source of problems at this layer.
4. **Transport Layer:** This layer represents the monitoring of transmissions between devices. If something is lost, it requests that the missing information be sent again.
5. **Session Layer:** In most cases, data is not able to be sent in just one "envelope." The session layer monitors the transmission of all the envelopes. When all the packets of information have been accounted for, the session is terminated.
6. **Presentation Layer:** This layer takes all the data out of the envelopes and creates a computer file that the user's computer application can understand. It is possible to transmit data of which the computer cannot make sense. The computer would then require another system that can read the data.

7. **Application Layer:** This is the layer with which the user interacts: the word processor, the Internet browser, and so on. Lots of things can go wrong here. Just because the file made it over doesn't means it will work. The file could contain a virus, be corrupted, or somehow be incompatible with the application that is attempting to use it.

In Chapter 21, we will use characteristics of the OSI model to isolate network problems. For now it is enough to understand that there is some logic to what's going on—or not going on.

Essential Network Components

The average network user never sees the majority of the equipment that connects things together. Switches, routers, hubs, firewalls, and file servers usually reside in air-conditioned locked rooms. The average user only sees the computers and printers with cables disappearing into the wall. Technologists have to know what happens after the wires disappear into the wall, but it is beneficial if everyone has a general understanding of the network's operation.

Network Interface Cards

The network starts at the NIC (Network Interface Card). The term *NIC* is a bit misleading because Most NICs are not cards; their functions are integrated into the PC's motherboard. The wireless equivalent of the NIC is called a WNIC—the W stands for *wireless*. In both cases, they are the point where data is transferred in and out of the networked device.

Network Cables

Network cables are the roads for data. The cabling infrastructure is in many ways the most important part of the network. First of all, it will probably be the longest lived part of your network. Because it is difficult to re-cable a building, cables may remain unchanged for ten, twenty, or thirty years. Time is not kind to cabling systems. Devices are constantly increasing in speed and demanding more from the physical wire. Wires in the walls may be damaged by workers pulling other types of line, students may yank on the cables often enough to damage the wall jacks, and your school's local family of mice may develop a taste for the cable's casing. Cable problems tend to be difficult to diagnose. Not only are the wires hidden from view but the type of errors they create often look like computer software or hardware problems.

Not long ago there was a wide variety of cable types that were in use. Today, the near total domination of Ethernet as a communications protocol has resulted in cable types being reduced to a few versions of twisted-pair cooper cables. *Twisted pair* is a term used to describe how the individual wires within a cable are twisted around each other so as to reduce interference. If the wires were not twisted, they would function as a form of radio antenna.

Cooper-based Ethernet cables use descriptors such "Type 5," "Type 5e," and "Type 6" cables (the term *type* is interchangeable with *cat*—short for *category*).

Very-high-speed connections usually use fiber-optic cables with their own set of descriptors. Fiber-optic cables may also be running Ethernet. With regard to the school environment, fiber-optic cables will probably only come into consideration when connecting buildings on a school campus. Fiber-optic cables are great for connecting separated sites because they have the ability to run for miles without signal loss. Cooper cables, in contrast, are rated for 300 meters. Fiber is also commonly used to connect high-end switches together or to connect to powerful servers. The cost of fiber optics is still significantly higher than that of cooper, so it is only used when specifically required.

Below are some considerations to keep in mind when dealing with network cabling.

1. All cables have distance limitations. Even fiber-optic cables have distance limitations that come into play when you're next laying a transoceanic cable. Type 5 cables have a distance limit of 300 meters. To go beyond 300 meters the signal must be rebroadcast by a network switch or some other powered device. It's important to remember that while anything within 300 meters is supposed to function to specifications, devices that operate at close to the technical specifications may not achieve full performance as the distance approaches 300 meters. It's also true that a low-speed connection may work fine at 350 meters. It's just that you never want to design any system beyond its limits because you never know what you will want to do with your network next year.

2. Each cable is rated for a maximum speed. The speed requirements of your network will vary depending on what is being connected. The less expensive Type 5 is fine for connecting typical desktop PCs while more expensive cabling should be considered for servers, connections between network switches, and computers used for multimedia creation.

3. Each cable type requires that the cable be installed in a specific manner. For example, if you bend a Type 5 cable around a sharp corner, the cable is not considered Type 5. The physical properties of the cable and the installation method are combined in the definition of a cable type.

4. Ask about fire codes in your area. Cables that go through ceilings or walls often need to have a fireproof casing. Naturally, this is more expensive than the typical PVC plastic casing, but not as expensive as running the cables through a metal conduit, the alternative fireproofing method.

5. Plan for the long term. Build in extra capacity. The price of adding extra lines during the initial construction is low when compared to the expense of adding new cables at a later point. Get a slightly faster cable if you can, and put in connections where a computer might go. You never know when teachers will move their desks or a supply closet will become your new network wiring room. If your school digs a trench between buildings for any reason, see if you can put in a fiber-optic line. Look for opportunities to increase infrastructural support when the cost to do so is low.

Figure 4. Hub Traffic Flow

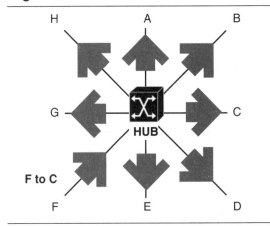

Hubs and Switches

Hubs and switches serve the same purpose—they connect network devices. Hubs, now found exclusively at the low end of the market, relay the signals from one wire to all the other wires connected to that hub. A switch serves the same purpose but also has intelligence built in that directs an incoming signal only to the wires for the devices that are to receive the signal. Switches make the network more efficient than hubs because each wire only carried the traffic destined for it. A hub, on the other hand, fills the wire with the traffic for all devices connected to that hub regardless of whether or not the data is relevant to the connected device. If your neighbor is transferring a large file, that transfer could consume your wire's capacity to the point of stopping your work. This isolation of traffic provided by a switch is a significant security benefit. With a hub, all the users could potentially capture the traffic destined for their neighbors. This technique of snooping is especially dangerous if your network transmits sensitive information in unencrypted form.

The good news about hubs and switches is that they look a lot more complicated than they are. In most cases, after the wires have been plugged in, the hubs and switches will function without problems for years.

Routers

A router connects different networks together. The most common example would be a connection to the Internet, but they are also used to connect separate LANs (Local Area Networks) together. Routers not only need to be configured with information about the networks it connects, but it actively monitors these connections to build a table, called a *routing table*, that describes the best routes for data to take.

Routers are far more difficult to configure than switches and hubs. Switches and hubs look complicated because of all their lights, but aren't; while routers look simple but aren't. If you've been confused by setting up a router, you're not alone. High-end routers have so many specialized configurations that it's normally best to hire a specialist.

At the low end, most routers are not even identified as routers. Any always-on connection to the Internet uses a router. Much public confusion over what a router is has to be placed at the doorstep of the broadband service providers. Knowing that their customers are former modem users, they label their routers as "cable modems" or "DSL modems." The term *modem* stands for "modulate/demodulate." A true modem takes digital data and turns it into sound—the fax-like screeching one hears at the start of a connection—and then converts incoming sound signals back into digital form. Today's broadband networks are completely digital in their operation, however, and thus require no conversion to sound. While the misleading

Figure 5. Switch Traffic Flow

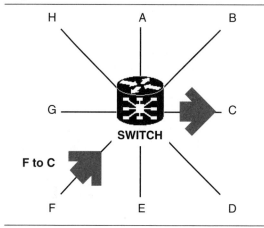

use of the term *modem* to mean a router may be helpful to the typical home user, it leads to confusion for the technical support person who asks to see the router only to be told that the school only has a modem.

Another source of confusion regarding routers is the fact that the router's core function of connecting different networks is often combined with auxiliary functions. Routers may combine some or all of the following: firewall, switch and hub, wireless access point, DHCP, and NAT (these two last terms will be explained in later chapters).

Firewalls

Firewalls serve as a barrier between a trusted side (your network) and an untrusted side (everyone else). While most firewalls are used to protect the local area network's (LAN) connection to the Internet, firewalls can and are used between LANs, within LANs, and on individual PCs. If there is a reason to keep someone out, a firewall is important to have.

As important as firewalls are, they aren't always used effectively. A sad fact of computer security is that attacks from the inside are as much a concern as attacks from outside the network.[1] While internal attackers may not be as technically sophisticated as international hackers, they know what is of value and by definition have access to the system. Ironically, most organizations have sophisticated forms of protection from external threats but are unaware of internal threats. Perhaps the reason is that a hacker in Russia is more interesting to portray in the movies or report on the local news than is a disgruntled employee or a bored student. Anyone responsible for the network's security does not have luxury of basing a security system on public perceptions.

There are many misperceptions regarding firewalls. The term *firewall* gives the impression that everything is kept out by a wall, when in reality it acts like a screen door. On simple networks, the firewall is normally configured to block all incoming traffic and allow all outgoing traffic, so traffic out of the local network is usually free to leave without restriction. Naturally, the firewall allows for traffic to come in that was originally requested from inside the network. This means that when a user visits a website, the firewall allows the website to send back the requested webpage.

Firewalls become tricky when a network includes a publicly accessible server, such as a web or email server. Public servers by their very nature require the firewall

---

1. *CSI/FBI Computer Crime and Security Survey*, by L. A. Gordon, M. P. Loeb, W. Lucyshyn, & R. Richardson. Computer Security Institute Publications, 2005, p. 15.

Figure 6. Typical Firewall

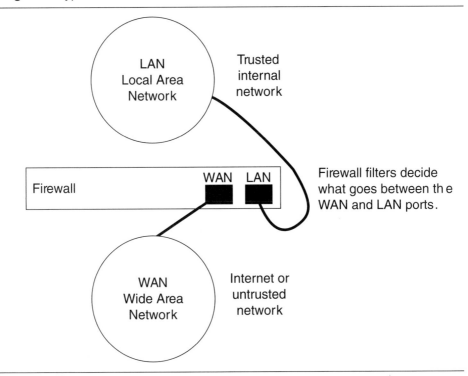

to allow public access, hackers included. That's not to say that a firewall becomes useless when a public server is introduced. It still protects your other computers and it can block traffic of the wrong type to the public server. It's a difficult concept, but every connection has multiple connection types called *ports*. Email, for example, might use port 25 while web traffic uses port 80. A firewall can allow approved communication types to pass through and block anything the user has not approved.

Hackers have adjusted to the ways in which firewalls operate and now focus on making attacks that appear to be legitimate email or web traffic. To use a metaphor, hackers see no reason to struggle with a locked front door if a first-floor window is left open. Of course, the "window" has to be left open if the "allowed" public is going to reach a given website or send in email messages. The hacker attempts to take advantage of security holes in the software that runs the public server. For example, a hacker may use a security hole in a web server system in order to gain control of the web server application. At the very least, they can bring down the web server or modify the web content. If they are lucky, they might even gain control over the entire server. Once that happens, the server can be used to attack other servers or the hacker can replace the login program with one that sends all the user names and passwords to the hacker.

The firewall vendors have recognized the fact that many attacks are coming in through the firewall quite legally. The answer to malicious people using open ports on the firewall is to use application level gateway filtering. An *application level gateway* is a system within the firewall that examines all the traffic coming in on a public port. If it sees a command that is invalid, it denies the connection. If the data is clean, it allows it to pass. Such systems are not without their weaknesses. Close inspection of all the data requires significant processing power, and attacks that have not yet been registered with the firewall vendor may get through.

DHCP (Dynamic Host Configuration Protocol)

Every network device requires a unique number and a variety of other addresses that help them function on the network. Assigning and configuring devices manually is time consuming and prone to errors. DHCP is a system that automates this chore.

Every network device has a unique identity called an IP number. Just as a telephone cannot communicate without a unique number, a network device must also have a unique number. Telephone numbers and IP numbers actually have a number of characteristics in common. The White House's fax number is 001-202-395-1232 and their website's IP number is 63.161.169.137. Both are represented in groupings of numbers. Each group represents a group within the group just above it. In the case of the telephone number, "001" is the country code for the United States and 202 is an area code for Washington, D.C. "395" is an exchange within the 202 area code and "1232" is a number in that exchange. The same logic applies to the IP address. There is one fundamental difference between the two systems: telephone numbers always have the same number of digits and each digit can range from 0 to 9. IP addresses, on the other hand, always have four sets of numbers called "octets," but each group of numbers can be a number between 0 and 255.

DHCP servers work by assigning addresses to devices by maintaining a pool of available numbers. As a network device without an IP address starts up it searches the network for a DHCP server. It talks to the DHCP server and at the end of the process it has an IP address. These IP numbers are described as dynamic address because they are provided dynamically and may change the next time the device communicates with the DHCP server. While it is possible to have the DHCP server assign a device with a fixed or "static" IP number that never changes, most systems provide IP addresses that will change. The frequency of change is governed by a setting called *time to life*. This setting is essentially a clock that starts when the device is off or disconnected. If the device does not reappear on the network before the time has expired, it must obtain a new IP number. There are two reasons for this. The first is that rotating IP numbers can serve as a security measure because anyone outside the network will not know the device's current address. The second reason is that a device may break or otherwise not be on the network again and that the number that was assigned it should be released back into the pool of available numbers.

When the DHCP server is running properly, there is little you have to do. However, when it freezes or has been turned off, the devices on your network will start losing their numbers as their time-to-live periods expire. It's an easy problem to spot, as computers start to lose their connections to the network in the order in which they obtained their dynamic number. Normally, the solution is to restart the DHCP server and all will fix itself in short order. Larger networks should have multiple DHCP servers.

2

Network Architectures

When was the last time you saw a house with marble columns built on sand or an entrance to a baseball stadium only big enough for one person at a time to enter? Some things go together while other things do not. Designing an effective network architecture for your school is all about making sure all the elements go together.

It's easy to overlook the compatibility between network elements because it's rare to purchase an entire network from a single vendor. So it's easy to get lost in the comparison between printer X and printer Y, meanwhile losing sight of overall system. Obviously, it's critical that all the components function together. What is less obvious is the attention that needs to be given to bottlenecks. A bottleneck can be defined as the limiting factor for a system. The topic of what a bottleneck is and how to handle it is very important to designing a network architecture.

Bottlenecks

You can never go wrong buying the most powerful computer, router, switch, and so forth—unless, of course, you have a budget. Frequently you will hear from novice computer buyers, "I didn't plan on getting the $3,000 dollar computer, but the sales guy said I needed it and it certainly does work great." Unfortunately for the buyer, a $1,500 dollar unit might have worked just as well. In this case, the user is the system's bottleneck. He is the bottleneck because he is unable to use the additional power of the unit above $1,500. No matter how fast he types his letters and email messages, a $1,500 computer will be just as instantaneous in its response as would be a $3,000 computer. In fact, his spending the additional $1,500 on hardware may have resulted in his keeping his dial-up account to the Internet rather than installing a broadband connection. Saving money on the computer and spending it on the broadband connection would have been a very good trade-off because the money would have gone toward the element that does impact the user's effectiveness.

Sales people sometimes suggest that that extra money spent on their product is really an investment because it offers "room for growth." This claim is misleading. Most people don't feel comfortable upgrading their computers, and thus the ability to do so is usually a wasted option. Furthermore, computers are usually designed so that all the components work well together. Adding a new video card to your system 4 years down the line is not going to improve your video performance if the motherboard on the computer was designed to support the maximum speed of the original video card.

Bottlenecks are good or bad depending on the trade-off that is made. In the case of the user who paid $3,000, he did not realize that his being a bottleneck made the additional $1,500 a bad investment. He also did not take into consideration that dial-up access to the Internet was actually a bottleneck worth spending money on.

A good bottleneck is one where all the components match each other, so that you are not paying for excess capacity. So for an already optimal configuration, purchasing a better component would not gain much because the other parts of the system would not be able to take advantage of its faster speed. A bad bottleneck, on the other hand, is where money is invested in parts of the system that cannot benefit from the extra capacity. Let's take a car as an example of optimal configuration. Adding performance-racing tires to an old station wagon would not be a good use of money because the car would not handle significantly better. However, putting racing tires on a racing car that currently has tires designed for a station wagon would make a great difference.

You have two options when confronted with a suboptimal configuration: push back the bottleneck by investing more so that the other parts are better utilized, or scale down the underutilized parts. This constant seesawing between bottlenecks applies to every technology decision. All the bottlenecks of computer network have to be matched so that the optimal balance can be achieved. Within each area of the network there will be specific sets of bottlenecks. The network infrastructure has one set, each computer has its own set, and specialized subsections such as multimedia labs and libraries have their own sets. Naturally, all this balancing is done within the context of the ultimate bottleneck: budget.

Peer-to-Peer Network Architecture

Peer-to-peer networking has gained much recent publicity due to all the music-sharing networks. There are many types of peer-based networks, but the defining quality is that users on the network directly communicate with each other as equals or "peers." Sometimes there is a centralized server that coordinates these connections, but the result is always the connection between peers. Let's compare a common form of peer-to-peer networking, file sharing, with server-based download sites. Users of file-sharing networks are sending files—usually music files—directly between themselves; whereas download sites, such as Apple's music store, have staff placing files on a server from which users can then download. There is no direct connection between the staff member's computer and that of the users.

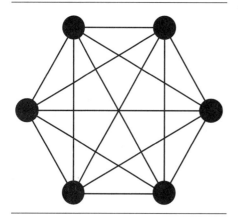

Figure 7. Peer-to-Peer Model

Peer-to-peer networks were popular in the early days of school networks because dedicated computer servers were too expensive. For a small network, purchasing a separate computer just to share resources didn't make economic sense. If you had a network with five computers, each costing $2,000, the adding of a sixth unit for the sole purpose of acting as a server would be equivalent to adding $400 to the price of each of the five other computers. Those days are over. Hardware costs are low enough that dedicating computers to specialized purposes makes economic sense.

Peer-to-peer systems have a number of disadvantages. First, they require that all shared computers be turned on. If the school's attendance database is on the secretary's computer and he is out of sick, and thus did not turn on his computer, no one else can have access to it. Second, some shared computers might get so much activity as to make them unusable to their primary users. For example, if three users are using the database located on a fourth computer, the person on the fourth computer may find his computer unusable at that time.

Peer-to-peer technology has found new life with the rise of operating systems such as Linux. For example, people using Linux on their servers can use Microsoft's peer-to-peer networking technology—referred to as *sharing*. Because Linux, as well as many other operating systems, have the ability to interoperate with Microsoft's peer-to-peer technology, people using Linux-based servers can make their servers appear to be peers on the Windows-based network. The users keep their familiar Windows desktop while the school saves money on the servers.

Peer-based networks are now coming back. Programs such as Groove allow networks of computers to function as a virtual server. In the days of slow computers with little disk space, this model would not have been appealing. Modern computers have so much excess capacity that running a server that may be handling dozens of simultaneous users is not as problematic as it once was. So, whereas in the past the goal of peer-to-peer networks was to eliminate the need for a server, today's peer-to-peer networks take advantage of the fact that most computers have the excess power to function as servers in addition to performing the routine user-level applications.

Systems like Groove get around some of the traditional problems of the old peer-to-peer networks by copying data to more than one computer. This means that turning off a computer does not have to shut down an important resource, nor does one computer shoulder the entire burden. The peer-to-peer system actively monitors the network's performance and redirects users to the least busy computers.

One of the attractive features of the new peer-based networks is the flexibility they afford. A group can share materials and create communication systems as needed. The group disbands when the project is done and the group's members reform into other groupings as needed. As with all new paradigms, these new peer-to-peer systems are still finding their place in the educational matrix. Undoubtedly, these new networks will be created for doing ad hoc projects. The main problem with them in an educational context is that they are more difficult to monitor; thus, student privacy can be an issue when you don't know who's on the network or even that there is a network.

Server-Based Networks

Server-based networks are those where one or more computers are dedicated to being a server. Examples of servers are file servers, web servers, email servers, etc. In the peer-to-peer model, every computer on the network might act as a server in addition to its primary duties as a desktop. It did not take long before users of heavily accessed desktop units threw up their hands and demanded another

Figure 8. Server Model

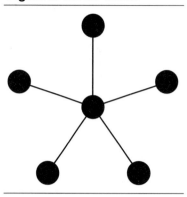

computer—leaving the original computer to function as a dedicated server.

Once a computer has been dedicated as a server, the characteristics that make it a good desktop system are no longer important. In the 1980s, low-end servers were often nothing more than powerful desktops. Those days are gone. While it is true that most servers are more powerful than desktop units in one or more characteristics, it is not true that they are always more powerful than their desktop kin. For example, servers rarely have a need for a good monitor to be connected. Over time, the hardware and software for servers evolved from powerful desktop units to general-purpose servers, and finally to the myriad of specialized server types. An email server is different from a web server, as is a database server different from a file server. Even within server types, such as web servers, the specific requirements can greatly affect the hardware used.

In the next section we will take a look at the characteristics of some common server types.

File Server

A file server is essentially a big hard disk. It must have enough hard disk space for all the school's data. A close second in importance to storage capacity is the hard disk's access speed. There are many measurements of access speeds, but the bottom line is that when multiple users ask for their files, the file server needs to find and deliver it to the user within an acceptable time period. It's difficult to say what an "acceptable time period" is, but a good rule of thumb is probably the time it takes to load a file off the typical user's local hard disk.

Access speed for a file server is based primarily on the speed of the hard disks and the speed of the network connections between the file server and the user. In a typical network one might have 50 users on a file server with each using having a 10 megabits/second network connection. Potentially, if every user downloaded a large file at the same time, the server could be hit with almost a total of 500 meg/second requests. While it's rare for everyone to download large files at the same time, it can happen for a variety of reasons. For example, students in the multimedia lab start class by opening all their video files or an announcement is sent out telling users to download the latest security patch before going on the Internet. A more likely scenario would be a network with a few heavy users—such as a desktop publisher who regularly opens up very large graphic files. During these file transfers the other users may find that the network is at its maximum capacity. Essentially, the network has a traffic jam. If money were not an issue, the solution would be to add more capacity to the network connection. Given that adding capacity requires money, another solution may be needed. For example, set a policy stating that staff on the first floor should access the security patch between 10 and 12 o'clock and staff on the second floor between 12 and 2 o'clock. As for the desktop publisher, it may be more economical to install a read/writable DVD drive on the local computer than it would be to upgrade the file server and the network connections.

The good news with file servers is that they don't require much processor speed: finding and sending files doesn't require a lot of "thinking" on the part of the computer. Once again, the issue of bottlenecks comes into play. A more powerful computer isn't necessarily going to increase speed. Generally, putting one's money into very fast and large hard disks is the way to go.

Email Server

Email servers don't require a great deal of power or storage space if they are used exclusively for sending and receiving email. In this role, the email server is only holding the message until it can be delivered. The biggest storage space requirement for this type of email server will be for all the log files. Most servers log almost every action it takes. Novice administrators not knowing this can allocate too little disk space to later find their system frozen due to log files consuming all the space.

Many email servers also function as group schedulers, contact databases, online email folders, and file storage areas. While the standard email server can run on even the most basic hardware, these multifunctional email servers can quickly consume hardware at a dizzying rate. It is not uncommon for a school to install a multifunctional email server expecting it to be a traditional email server with a few bells and whistles. Later, they realize that the bells-and-whistles features have sucked the life out of the hardware and are now imperiling the email system. The most typical result is an emergency upgrade that is both expensive and awkward.

There are two basic philosophies for handling email. The first is for the email server to operate as a post office, where the user comes and collects the email. Collected email is subsequently removed from the server. This system if often referred to as "POP email." This is the type of system that ISPs (Internet Service Providers) typically offer to customers. These systems run well on inexpensive equipment.

The second philosophy of email server operation is to have it function as both the post office and as a storage facility. The email continues to reside on the server until the user deletes it. The two most common email systems in this category are IMAP and Microsoft Exchange. Most email clients can support having multiple email accounts on a variety of email server types. It's when one starts to use the advanced features, such as calendaring, that one's choice of email client becomes limited.

The post office system (i.e., POP) works well when money is tight and the user is not going to be accessing the email from multiple computers. Correspondingly, the second system (i.e., IMAP and Exchange) is good for users who will be accessing their accounts from multiple computers, because the email remains on the server. This means that when the user uses another computer, the user will see all the stored email. In contrast, POP systems download messages and the user cannot see those downloaded messages from another computer. Anyone building a server of the second type should plan for large storage capacity and ample processor power.

Web Server

Web servers, like email servers, can be simple or extremely complicated. As any dietitian will tell you, it's not the potato that is fattening; it's all the additions that expand the waistline. A website for a small organization does not require a powerful computer. In fact, web servers can be found in small network devices, printer server boxes, for example. In fact, one manufacturer has found a way to incorporate a web server into an otherwise normal toaster.

A basic web server is not too different from a file server in its basic functioning. The difference with a file server is that a web server usually does not require as much storage space and access speed is not so much of an issue because the speed of the Internet is usually a limiting factor. Both servers keep track of files and send them to the user as required. Web servers are all about sending files to the user's browser.

Once all the files are on the user's system, the browser constructs the webpage. Because browsers can interpret the component files in different ways, the author of the webpage doesn't necessarily know what the user will see. This apparently odd behavior is required by the fact that the web designer has no idea what type of hardware and software settings will be used to view the website. The browser acts as a translator between the site's instructions and the user's equipment. While most sites will display as the designer intended, there will be situations where the browser will alter the appearance of the site. In one unfortunate website design the designers for a church website decided to use a deep red color as the background color. The problem was that some systems shifted the color to a blood red. Luckily for them, one of the reviewers of the prototype site kept referring to the site as "satanic" in appearance—not what they were going for!

Most large websites dynamically create their webpages. *Dynamic* means the webpage that a user sees is constructed at the time of user's request for the page by taking content from some type of database and inserting it into a design template. Dynamic content creation is very useful when the pace of updates would be too rapid for manual editing or when creating customized webpages. CNN's website, for example, determines which part of the world a user is from and then creates a page that for the user's region. Or, in the case of Google's news site, users can customize which sections they read and how those sections are organized on the page. The server dynamically collects the stories in which the user has expressed interest and organizes them within the structure that the user has designed. On a less pleasant note, dynamic servers allow commercial sites to display advertisements targeted specifically to the visitor. So, if the user purchased a set of knitting needles last time, perhaps it will display ads for yarn on the user's next visit.

High-end web servers are in fact multiple servers. In many cases, a website may well be a collection of multiple servers tied together produce the website. Typical elements are:

- **Web server:** The two most common web servers are Apache and Microsoft's Internet Information Server. This is all that is required to run a website with static webpages.
- **Middleware:** Programs such as Cold Fusion, PHP, Microsoft's ASP, and Tomcat are applications that manage the interface between what the web server sends to the user's browser and the sources of data to which it has access.

- **Database server:** MySQL, Oracle's database, and Microsoft's SQL are some of the major databases used to store web content and user information. The data they contain are accessed by the middleware applications and delivered to the user via the web server.
- **Application servers:** Websites using interactive elements or multimedia may use servers such as Macromedia's Flex or Microsoft's Media Server. These servers are called on either by the stand-alone server or by the middleware server to provide content directly to the user. For example, the user clicks on an icon representing a video and the video server directly communicates with the user.
- **Authentication servers:** Servers such as Kerberos, Radius, and Microsoft's Active Directory are all used to assure that the user is who she or he says she or he is. This is obviously very important if it's a student checking grades or finding out how much is due for tuition.
- **Log server:** Websites generate huge amounts of information. Some information is used to record the status of all the various services, and lots of statistics are kept on usage patterns. These logs can become huge and the analysis of the usage patterns can take significant amounts of time. Large systems often move these logging features of a separate unit to reduce the strain on the web server.

One note that should be added to this discussion of servers is that the term *server* does not necessarily imply an individual hardware device. Multiple servers can run on the same computer. While it is possible to combine email servers with file servers, people do not tend to do this because of the different set of bottlenecks that comes with each service.

Database Server

The majority of the world's data resides in a computer database—in fact, most of which is sitting on a mainframe computer.[2] Most databases function with the same fundamental components. Information is stored in compartments called *fields*. An example of information that might go into a field would be a telephone number. All the fields associated together, such as a person's contact information, make a record. All the records together are called a *database table*. The data is typically comprised of information such as names, addresses, and other facts, but it can just as well contain multimedia files.

A single database may have multiple tables that relate to one another. This is called a *relational database*. A database with one table is referred to as a *flat database*. There are two other important terms to know: *record ID* and *indexes*. Every record has to be unique. Databases take care of this requirement by automatically recreating a unique record ID. So the first record is labeled "1" and the second one "2." Really bad things happen when tables with the same IDs are merged without

---

2. IBM's "dinosaur" turns 40. PCs were supposed to kill off the mainframe, but Big Blue's big boxes are still crunching numbers, *San Francisco Chronicle*'s SFGate.com, by B. Pimentel, April 5, 2004.

Table 1. Database Table Structure

Record 1	Field 1	Field 2	Field 3	Field 4	Field 5
Record 2	Field 1	Field 2	Field 3	Field 4	Field 5
Record 3	Field 1	Field 2	Field 3	Field 4	Field 5
Record 4	Field 1	Field 2	Field 3	Field 4	Field 5

reconciling ID numbers. Having multiple records with the same ID numbers is like a telephone system with multiple locations with the same telephone number.

A database index can be thought of as a preordered list. The database can be instructed to constantly sort one or more columns. A column in Table 1 would be all the Field 1s. Indexes are very helpful when the database frequently organizes information within a specific field. For example, it is common to index the last name field in a contact database because users often want to see the names in alphabetical order and to be able to search quickly for someone based on their last name. However, indexes can be taken to extreme. More is not better. Having the database index every field can result in severely degrading the database's performance with few practical benefits.

A database server is a computer dedicated to the operation of one or more databases. Database servers can require substantial computer power when required to manipulate databases and/or to serve multiple users simultaneously. In other words, databases can become very expensive. This is especially true when the information being stored is either very sensitive in nature or mission critical. *Mission critical* is generally defined as any process that would bring operations to a halt if it were inaccessible—or any system that your boss has a particular interest in. Generally, in a school, the mission critical databases, such as student records and staff payroll, are handled by district offices or by third parties.

3

Operating Systems

Deciding which operating system to use can take on an almost religious fervor. As much as others may tell you otherwise, any operating system can do the majority of functions you are likely to want done. We'll take a look at how to pick an operating system.

Putting the Horse Before the Cart

Too often people buy the hardware and software before deciding what the equipment should do. It doesn't matter if you think Open Source software, like Linux, is a great value if it cannot run a specific program you must use.

Another common mistake is to design systems for improbable uses that dramatically raise the design specifications. For example, someone might say, "Wouldn't it be nice if all the computers could handle real-time video editing?" Well, that would definitely be nice, but it would also add another thousand or two dollars to the price of each unit. A much better solution would be to buy a few dedicated graphic workstations.

"Let's plan for future needs" is another often-heard phrase. It sounds very reasonable. If you're really going to need it, shouldn't you plan for it now? With computer prices constantly going down, you may find that buying extra capacity now simply isn't as economical as buying it later. This, of course, assumes that you will require extra capacity at a later point—you may not. For the last few years, even the cheapest computer is able to run most standard applications. Given that it is unlikely that word processing is going to become vastly more demanding on computer resources, it is fairly safe to assume that if the applications you use now run fine on your system, they will continue to do so 3 to 5 years down the line. The exceptions to this rule are for computers that run video editing and desktop publishing. These systems can never get enough power. Adding some extra hardware now can indeed extend the useful life of these units. Even with the high-end computers you can plan for future expansion. For instance, you could plan to add more memory and

Figure 9. OS Diagram

a second processor chip to your multimedia computers in the next budget year. Not only does this spread the financial pain between two budget cycles, but the prices for memory and processor chips will most likely be significantly cheaper. Of course, you need to be aware that 5 years later the process chip you want to add may no longer be sold.

One of the best ways to design a network is to visit someone else who already has a network doing things similar to what you want to have. If their system is good, copy it. There is no arguing with success.

Picking the Right Operating System

All the major operating systems are so full-featured that listing your system requirements will probably not eliminate any of them. The only real sticking points tend to be mandated software applications. Some programs only run on certain operating systems. If you must run a specific program that only runs on Windows, your number of choices decreases to one. While it is true that you don't have to use the same operating system everywhere, standardization of software and hardware is a highly desirable goal. Below are some of the factors you should consider when picking an operating system.

- **Cost of purchase:** The true cost of an operating system is not always obvious because large sites and educational or nonprofit sites can frequently obtain attractive discounts from Microsoft and Apple. While Linux can be obtained for free, the big vendors, such as Red Hat, actually charge for their commercial versions of Linux. Having the commercial version of Linux can be important for obtaining certain forms of support.
- **Cost of operation:** Cost of operation can be determined by multiplying the expected frequency of trouble by the cost of getting the problems fixed. Operational costs can overwhelm the cost of even the more expensive purchases.
- **Multiple operating systems versus a single system:** A key decision is whether to have more than one operating system in your school. There are cost and security considerations that must be considered. Diversity of systems can increase security because an attack may only affect one form of technology. Of course, if you install systems you don't understand, that is a security problem that probably offsets any increase you gained from diversity.
- **Security:** How much security do you need? No system is absolutely secure, but some are better than others, due either to their inherent security capabilities or the fact that hackers don't target them as frequently.
- **Third-party support:** Some systems may seem less expensive initially but require additional purchases. An operating system cannot be isolated from the hardware and supporting software required to make it perform the functions you expect of it.
- **Application support:** Do mandated programs run well on the operating system? Some vendors put out applications for a primary operat-

ing system and then issue versions for other operating systems at a later date—and perhaps with less attention to detail.

- **Hardware requirements:** Saving a few hundred dollars on an operating system doesn't mean much if the required hardware is thousands more. This cost factor is not limited to the hardware on which it runs; you also have to consider the cost of peripherals, such as printers and scanners.
- **User training:** Will your users feel comfortable with the system? Anything that reduces training and support costs is a very good thing. Not only is training costs a major factor but user perceptions of a new system can make or break its success.

There are, of course, other factors. For example, many organizations have a restricted vendor list or refuse to support certain hardware and software platforms.

The Big Three

Microsoft is the proverbial 800-pound gorilla when it comes to operating systems. Apple has long had a strong position in the education market. Linux is the upcoming operating system. No single operating system is always best, and all three systems are able to work together on the same network.

Windows

The courts have declared Microsoft to be a monopoly, and users often talk about its "monolithic" operating system. While it is true that all of Microsoft's operating systems are called "Windows," there are at least a dozen versions of Windows, and the difference between versions such as Windows CE, Windows 95, and Windows Vista are vast.

The Windows system is generally a permissive operating system in that it allows for applications running on it to work together. This is a nice feature when you want to send email messages out through a Word mail merge via Outlook or you want a new software package to install automatically. The downside of convenience is that it also makes life easier for virus writers and hackers. While many of the Microsoft's famous security bugs are the result of programming errors, many security issues are in fact features abused by hackers.

Cost is one of the most contentious issues surrounding operating systems. Microsoft says that Windows is less expensive than free operating systems such as Linux because it is so easy to install and to maintain that the initial purchase price is more than offset by savings in labor and support. Apple makes the same claims with regard to the less expensive Windows. All three operating systems provide attractive academic discounts.

Apple's OS X

Apple has long focused on the educational market. Their claim to fame has always been that their operating system is easy to use. This is quite a feat when one considers that their current operating system, OS X, is built on a none-too-friendly version of UNIX called BSD (Berkeley Software Distribution). UNIX is what Linux is modeled after. UNIX is a powerful operating system created by Bell Labs back in the '60s and '70s.[3] Today, UNIX is frequently found on high-end servers and mainframes.

While the ease-of-use gap between Apple's OS X and Microsoft's Windows has been closing—some would say because Microsoft imitates Apple's products—the advantage still goes to Apple. Schools using Apple computers claim that their support costs are much lower than they would be with a Windows environment because the users intuitively understand the Apple system, the hardware is of better quality, and the overall better security of the operating system means less time is spent applying security patches and fighting viruses.

One of the advantages Apple has traditionally enjoyed is its ability to control both the software and hardware elements. This is a significant advantage because many software problems are actually miscommunications between different elements of the system. When one can control all the elements, the potential for miscues is greatly reduced. Microsoft has started to enjoy these advantages via their issuing of technical specifications for hardware vendors to follow.

Apple computers are at a disadvantage to Microsoft-based computers in terms of the numbers of applications they can run. While this is not an issue for most tasks, there are situations where specific software programs only run on the Windows platform. It should be noted that it is possible to run Windows programs on the Mac using Windows emulation software. Emulation software makes the Windows program think it's running on a Windows computer. Some Macs include a PC card that essentially creates a PC computer within the Mac. Emulation and add-on PC cards both have advantages and disadvantages. Emulation is less expensive than a PC card but it is significantly slower and prone to flaky behavior.

Linux

Linux is a UNIX-like operating system. It evolved in the early 1990s in an effort to bring the power of UNIX to the personal computer. At that point, UNIX only ran on powerful hardware. Since its inception by a Finish college student, Linux has gained tremendous popularity due to power, flexibility, and free-cost structure. Linux and OS X have much in common because of their shared link to UNIX. While Linux is primarily associated with the server environment and OS X with the desktop, they can swap roles quite easily.

The Linux interface (actually, there are many possible interfaces) has dramatically improved. Linux is still stronger in its server role, but it is currently a viable solution on the desktop for the people using email, web browsing, and other routing software applications. Most users can transition a Linux desktop easily. The main limitation with Linux desktops is the ability to run some desktop programs. Most anything that can be done Windows and OS X–based desktops can be accomplished on a Linux-based desktop, but it may not be with the program of choice or with the same degree of ease. Linux, and to some extent OS X, have the problem of

---

3. The Creation of the UNIX Operating System, 2005, Available at http://www.bell-labs.com/history/unix/

having to maintain strict compatibility with Windows-based systems. Microsoft, on the other hand, does not have this problem and in fact even makes life difficult for outsider programs to be compatible with Microsoft products by constantly redefining the standards to which programs must adhere.

Of course, the best advantage for Linux is that it can be obtained at no cost. Like OS X, it has few security concerns and a reputation for reliability. Linux servers often run for years without failing or even requiring a reboot. The problem with supporting Linux is that its difficulty makes it a challenge to repair or modify. While there are many firms offering Linux support contracts, the paradox of software support is that the less an organization pays for something, the less they will be willing to spend on support. Getting your boss to purchase a 5,000-dollar-a-year support contract for a 40,000-dollar program is easy, but getting the same $5,000 to support a free Linux-based system is a hard sell. Therefore, Linux users frequently get their support from public forums on the Internet that are dedicated to Linux. If you have a technical background, these forums can be great, but the less technical may find these forums to be like the old adage about traveling abroad with a Berlitz book—you can ask questions but may not understand the answers.

OS Comparison Chart

Table 2 is a general comparison of how Apple OS X, Linux, and Microsoft Windows compare. The scale is not scientific, nor does it take into account special situations where the results might be different. After the chart, there is a brief description of each measurement criteria and the rationale for the rankings.

Table 2. OS Comparison Chart

	Linux	OS X	Windows
Purchase Price	1	3	2
Support Costs	2	1	3
Ease of Use	3	1	2
Number of Desktop Applications	3	2	1
Number of Server Applications	2	3	1
Security	1	2	3
Hardware Costs	1	3	2

Purchase Price

Linux is free or close to free depending on the distribution or "distro." A distro is a version of Linux that a company or group creates to meet a set of objectives they want to accomplish. Red Hat, Fedora, Debian, and Slackware are all examples of major Linux distros. Some require payment while other distributions are completely free. Windows and OS X are about the same in price. The upper hand goes to Windows because Apple's upgrades tend to be pricey. Remember that educational institutions and nonprofits can be eligible for substantial discounts. Factoring in deep discounts could result in Linux being the most expensive option. It's rare, by the way, to actually pay the list price for a system. Larger institutions can negotiate site licenses that can reduce list prices to less than 1/10 of list price. Unfortunately, if your school is small, you'll come much closer to paying list price.

Support Costs

OS X is perhaps the easiest operating system to support. Linux is perhaps even more trouble-free than OS X, but when something goes wrong it can be more difficult to fix. Even if support information can be found for free on the Internet, the skills to carry out the solution can be daunting.

Ease of Use

OS X is still considered to have a lead over Windows, though that lead has shrunk over recent years. Linux has perhaps made the most significant gains, but OS X and Windows are moving targets. The gap has narrowed greatly over the last few years but Windows still has a clear lead over Linux, as does OS X over Windows. Now that all three operating systems function on the same Intel-based computer hardware, comparisons and the competition between the three systems should increase.

Desktop Applications

Linux is trying to gain on Windows and OS X. Where it might be argued that OS X–based applications are easier than their Windows counterparts, it all depends on what one needs. For simple word processing, email, and Internet browsing, all three operating systems provide adequate tools. Windows has to be given the overall edge in this category because of its far greater number of applications.

Server Applications

This is the trickiest category to judge. OS X could be considered to be first if one takes into account that it can run most UNIX-based programs in addition to OS X-specific applications. Windows has a vast collection of server programs and can run a wide assortment of servers originally designed for the UNIX/Linux world. Linux is commonly considered the best value in the server realm.

Servers operating on the Internet are predominately running a set of programs referred to as LAMP, for Linux, Apache, MySQL, Perl/Python/PHP. Linux is the operating system. Apache is the web server. MySQL is a database application especially effective for supporting websites. The p stands for one of three popular scripting languages—good thing they all start with p. All the components in LAMP are Open Source and available at no charge. The popularity of the LAMP package on the Internet means that the individual components are constantly being optimized for performance and stability within the LAMP environment.

Security

Linux and OS X are both excellent in terms of security. (The truly paranoid should consider a cousin to Linux and OS X called OpenBSD.) Windows, however, isn't famous for security but it can be improved with additional effort. The bottom line is that a well-configured weak operating system is stronger than a missconfigured strong operating system. So if your school has a great deal of expertise with Windows and none with Linux, the installation of Linux may reduce security. There is also an argument that says that having multiple operating systems in an environment provides greater protection than that provided by a homogeneous environment. The counterpoint is that multiple operating systems may increase the environment's complexity to the point that the staff misses taking security precautions that they would have otherwise noticed. How this issue is handled depends greatly on your school's environment and skill sets.

Hardware Costs

Linux is the clear leader here. For example, its ability to turn an old desktop computer into an effective email server for is very compelling anyone on a limited budget. While one can argue that OS X's hardware is better quality than what is used in Linux or Windows systems, the up-front costs are still a factor to people on tight budgets.

The Browser as Operating System

With the advent of the Internet browser there have been repeated calls for the browser to replace the role of the traditional operating system. The basic idea is that web service providers would create applications on their systems that would replace the need for software applications to be stored on the local computer. In its fullest stage, the user would only need enough of an operating system to make the browser work. Naturally, this is a potential nightmare for Microsoft and for Apple because the functionality of their operating systems would no longer matter.

While web-based email systems have come close to being able to replace a PC-based email program, replacing word processing and database work has been more difficult to accomplish. Three factors are required before there can be a total transfer of software program functionality to the web. First, connection speeds have to be high. The connection's reliability is also vital. Second, the ability to customize is important. Most people do not customize their email systems, but most database workers do undertake extensive customization. Third, security has to be assured at every level. When millions of credit card numbers are being compromised on a regular basis, it naturally brings up concerns of how well protected your school's records might be.

Figure 10. Ajax Operation Model

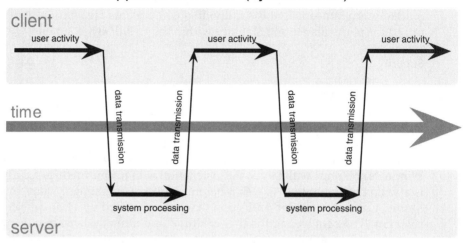

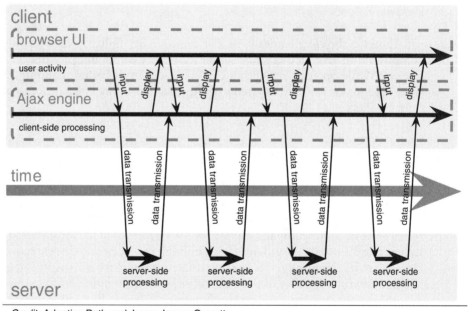

Credit: Adaptive Path and Jesse James Garrett

At present, some functions on the PC can be safely transferred to a browser-based system. With the increasing implementation of AJAX (Asynchronous JavaScript and XML), a new programming paradigm, the ability for other functions to work over the Internet has been greatly enhanced. Whether it will ever be enough to replace all the functions currently on the desktop remains to be seen, but it is a possibility worth considering.

4

Network Design Attack Plan

Attempting to implement a major new technology plan in a school automatically qualifies one for underdog status. This chapter will use the analogy of the guerrilla fighter, because he is a classic example of an underdog who frequently prevails. Guerrilla fighters are effective when they know the lay of the land, know the enemy, understand the fundamental principles of guerrilla warfare, and can lead a ragtag assortment of soldiers. School technologies working on low budgets have to do much the same thing. They don't have the luxury of making mistakes. There's no "Too bad that didn't work—let's buy the other system." A mistake stays around for a very long time—perhaps longer than the person who installed it. The rules of guerrilla warfare have many lessons worth learning.

Lay of the Land

The first step with any plan is to determine what the current situation is and what will be required. Too often, plans are either based on what someone else believes is a good plan or on reproducing the current network with new equipment. While it is a good idea to look at other people's networks, you should be careful that the specifics of your environment are addressed. Something as seemingly minor as a mandated software program—such as a school district budgeting system—can completely alter the technologies you are able to consider.

One of the most common mistakes technicians make is to take an exact measure of what the current network is doing so that the new network can be designed to do the exact same thing. This process does not take into consideration that the old system may not be working—it probably isn't if people want to replace it—or the possibilities offered by newer technologies. Every landscaper knows that they have to allow for growth when planting a sapling next to a house. Placing a young tree too close to the house results in it bending and distorting as it hits the side of the house. Many old networks are like trees planted too close to a house. Accommodations, stopgaps, and simply giving up become integral to the old network—some users many not even realize that these accommodations are a sign that something is wrong. To attempt to replace such a network based on an analysis of current needs is like the landscaper taking measurements of the old, distorted tree and replacing it with a new tree of the same shape to be planted in the same location. The landscaper should have made an assessment of the old tree to see what is healthy about it and what is not, and then plant a new tree in a nearby location where it has sufficient room to grow.

The best plans take into account the current operations, determine where important new activities are likely to develop in the school, and then match those requirements with the capabilities and trends in the external technological world. For example, the school may have a school-based radio station. They may want to replace their manual sound editing system with a computer-based system. A good plan will take into account that many radio stations are adding audio streaming over the Internet to their radio transmissions. Designing the system so that this option is available forestalls painful—read costly—redesign.

There are many ways to figure out current technical trends. One way is to ask people with systems similar to your proposed plan what they see coming down the road for them. Go to online discussion groups about the proposed network to see what themes are prevalent and find out what the group members are excited about. Visit the local computer trade show. If every booth has something related to wireless networking, you can be assured that this is going to be a significant trend in the coming year or so. Similarly, you definitely want to be concerned if the "next big thing" you've been told about by your technology vendor is nowhere to be seen at the show.

Avoiding Surprise

Technology is inherently complicated. Surprise comes in many forms and at any time. Here are some considerations when assessing risks—the surprise factor—in a plan.

- **Is there anything that is both unusual and very important?** If so, confirm that the other elements of the system function with the unusual part. The best way to do this is to call the technical support line regarding the "unusual" part and ask if there are known problems with the other programs and equipment in your plan. Ask technical support what they would consider to be the optimal system for their product. There is often a big difference between the specifications listed for "requirements" and those required for optimal performance. The requirements list is usually what is required to allow the product to function.
- **Does the plan depend heavily on one vendor?** If a vendor going out of business would jeopardize your operations, you had better check their financial health and the prospect that they might be acquired by a rival firm.
- **Are you the first person to discover a new way of doing things?** Sometimes a plan will incorporate a truly innovative feature—make sure you're innovative and not merely unique because everyone before you has either failed or found a better way.
- **Does the plan require the transformation of the organization?** Some organizational change should be expected, but large changes may not be welcomed by the users. Make sure everyone is onboard before casting off lines and sailing away.
- **Are there hidden costs?** Vendors may make their deals look attractive by selling at a lower price, knowing that you'll have to come back for something else. Make sure you know the expected costs over a num-

ber of years and don't assume "comes with a Microsoft software suite" means "Microsoft Office" and not the inferior "Microsoft Works"—or the free Microsoft WordPad.

- **Anything missing?** Be sure that a much cheaper price is not achieved through the use of pirated software. You should expect to have the master disks for anything installed on your system—and not just one copy for multiple computers. Software, especially hardware, has fairly low profit margins. In the case of software, the creator may even have listed retail prices that its retailers cannot go beneath. So, when a given price is far less expensive than all the other proposals, further research is required on your part.

Leading Your Ragtag Army

Don't be like the general who starts running across the field of battle only to find that his troops are watching from the trenches. Corporations have the ability to encourage support for a new system with training and extra technical support, while you'll have to rely solely on persuasion. Faculty tenure means your staff has the option of ignoring any system they don't want. Like a guerrilla army, the troops are either supportive or they go home.

The first thing to realize when attempting to build support for a new plan is to recognize that some staff may be impossible to persuade. You can hope they'll warm up to the new system once it's in place, but you should not count on it. Yet, on the other hand, don't write off or criticize hesitant staff members. A few will warm up when the new system starts to work. Those who continue to dislike the new system can often be convinced that the system, while not interesting to them, has some good points. In both cases, harsh words at the beginning will forfeit any hope of improvement when done.

Most people are inclined to support plans in which they feel involved. Since you cannot give everyone everything they want, you have to make it clear why some options were left out and others were kept. Keeping users informed eliminates a lot of "if only they had asked me" or "xyz system would have been much better." Still, however, you will find that even technological curmudgeons, who hate technology in all forms, can offer a meaningful opinion. Don't leave these people behind, too.

One caveat regarding sharing information with your users: don't cross the line between sharing information and looking indecisive and vacillating. Users will be fearful if they believe you don't know what you're doing. Even users who would otherwise support your plan will run for cover if they lose confidence in your ability to execute the plan. Where this line is depends on many factors: your personality, your relationships and reputation within the school, the size and importance of the project, and the history of how other decisions have been made within the school. Not everything needs to be shared with everyone. Initial discussions should probably be reserved for staff that you know to be open-minded and well informed. It's also important to ask for advice on those areas where the people you're asking are experts. For example, it's great to ask how a teacher would anticipate using a proposed program in their lesson plan, but if you simply ask what they think of the program in general it may seem that you don't know about the program. In other words, seeking input is good, whereas seeking assistance is not.

Where possible, create a system that works on multiple levels. Even the most uninterested staff member should have the potential to benefit. If you cannot take the curmudgeon to the mountain, bring him a few nice rocks. Never allow your toughest customers to feel that they are your opponent or the "loyal opposition." Design the system so that everyone can participate at some level. A corporation might be able to encourage compliance via pay raises or firings, but schools rarely offer meaningful incentives and few school administrators would take strong action against a good teacher solely for failing to support the technology plan.

A computerized attendance system is a perfect example of a system that could be sunk by one or two uncooperative teachers. Perhaps they refuse to use the system or they make so many mistakes that the resulting data is suspect. While you cannot force compliance, you are not helpless by any means. Assign a student to help the teacher take the attendance. Or have the teachers turn in their attendance reports via the old system and then have someone else input it. Once the holdouts see that the attendance lists are more accurate and faster, they'll be more open to taking the attendance with the new computerized system. Forcing the issue has little chance of success, and it may lock non-participating teachers into a position that they cannot back down from.

Never discount the fears of your toughest customers. It may well be that many others feel the same way but are so excited by the new system that they don't want to be to perceived as being critical. Fears like "What happens when this breaks in the middle of class?" or "Can a virus destroy all my students' projects?" are reasonable questions. If you don't have a good answer, get one. Many times, criticism highlights real problems that need to be fixed. It also never hurts to be perceived as being reasonable.

There are many forms of leadership. You have to get the official leaders to sign on to your network plan if you want funding, but you also need the support of the opinion leaders within the organization if you want to obtain broad support. Opinion leaders are typically the most popular individuals and the acknowledged "power users." A *power user* is someone with mastery of the current computer applications. Almost certainly there will be one or two individuals whose opinion will carry great weight. Hopefully, they won't be your curmudgeons.

Opinion leaders are accustomed to getting respect. Make sure that in your surveying of the school, you include their opinions. If they are agreeable, include them in reviewing any prototype system. If they have questions, make sure the questions are answered. If the opinion leaders are treated properly, the entire organization will be excited rather than anxious when the new system arrives.

Thinking Outside the Box

Sometimes the road most traveled is a toll road you cannot afford. And oftentimes there isn't a solution within your school's budget. You will have to think outside the box or perhaps look for a new box altogether. Being a creative genius is always nice in these situations, but barring that, you can apply a few steps to achieving out-of-the-box-dom.

1. **Make sure you're in the right box.** Don't start thinking out of the box before you're sure you're in the right box to begin with. Ask fundamental questions about every aspect of the plan. For example, is the video conference really required, or is it there because someone thought it was interesting? Does the school need both a computer lab and computers in the classrooms? Could a mobile cart of laptops replace the need for computers in multiple rooms? Does the typing class really benefit from computers or would typewriters work almost as well? And, just because it was done in the past should not be an automatic guarantee of inclusion in the new system.

2. **How many boxes are there?** Write down all the conceivable ways a given task can be done. Even off-the-wall ideas may lead to new ways of looking at things. Get people to brainstorm.

3. **Check out other people's boxes.** You always learn something from visiting someone else's network—even it's not the network you are planning to use.

4. **Sell your box to get a box.** Is there a grant or another source of money that would allow you to increase the resources available to you? Similarly, can you rent your "box" to others, such as an evening adult literacy project that meets in the school?

5. **Recycle your old box.** While the old system may not be meeting your needs, can some or all of it be recycled to serve the new network? Many times people associate the failure of the old system with the failure of all its parts. The old computers in the computer lab may be perfect for the typing class. Could you use the monitors from the old systems for the first year and then buy new monitors in the second year? You pay the same over time, but the costs are distributed between 2 years.

6. **Remember why you have the box.** It is all too easy to focus on the various aspects of the plan and forget the purpose of the plan. Having the plan's goals shift during the planning process can be a good thing if it's done intentionally. Just make sure the new goals are indeed better than the old goals and that everyone party to the planning recognizes that a shift has taken place. The last thing you want to hear at the end of the day is "that's not what we agreed to do."

5

Special Operations

It's rare for all the computers in the network to do exactly the same thing. A single school might contain a computer lab, classroom computers, library computer systems, administrative office computers, movable computer carts, and a multimedia lab. Buying computers that can do all these functions would make the entire system prohibitively expensive. Yet individualizing each computer creates additional support needs. The key is to standardize as much as you can and customize where needed.

Computer Labs

Uniformity of systems in a computer lab is a golden rule. Having one computer be better than the others is an invitation to students to rush for the good computers and avoid the less desirable units. Uniformity helps to assure that every student's experience will be the same. For the school technologist, uniformity is also important because makes it easier to diagnosis and fix problems.

Computer labs usually require mid-level computers. Higher-performance computers go to the multimedia lab. The lowest-performing computers go to the typing class. Over time, the computer lab may inherit the media lab's computers and in turn send its computers to the typing class. The quality level that is required is ultimately determined by the most demanding application the computer will commonly use. If Microsoft Publisher is the most demanding application in frequent use, then the systems need to be good enough to run it. Buying extra performance is often a waste of money that will force money to be cut from somewhere else.

It's the small things that will make the difference between a good lab and one that is constantly causing you problems. Here are a few steps to consider when designing a computer lab.

- **Order extra keyboards and mouse units.** These components will break frequently. If you're dealing with pre-K through third grade, you may want to get special keyboards that are tougher, smaller, and easier to clean.
- **Replace speakers with headphones.** Thirty computer speakers all going at the same time can be the proverbial Tower of Babel. If you plan on sharing each computer between two students you'll need two headphones and a line splitter. Otherwise, they'll be temped to flip over one of the earphones so that the other student can hear. The result will be broken headphones.

- **Install channel guides.** Channel guides cover the computer cables. It makes the lab cleaner and it makes it less likely that a student will accidentally pull out or trip over a cable. Be especially careful of wires that cross the floor.

- **Beware of user storage devices.** While most viruses are spread through email, there are many viruses that come through mobile storage devices, such as diskettes, read/writeable CD-ROMs, Zip disks, and USB devices (which include many MP3 music players). If you allow students to bring in these devices, you'll have a real security issue. Some computer labs mitigate this problem by ordering systems without floppy and Zip drives. Unfortunately, it is not so easy to do without USB and CD-ROM drives. For most schools, the main concern is still the diskette. Diskettes don't store as much as the other devices listed, but they have the great advantage of being cheap, small, and reusable. If the student wants a file, the computer lab teacher copies the file from a central computer. If that's going to be a frequent request, the best solution is to keep the floppy drives and make absolutely sure that your antivirus system is working. One thing to keep in mind if the computer lab teacher is transferring files off floppy disks: any infection of her or his computer will have the potential to infect all the data files to which she or he has access. A student, by comparison, can only infect the files to which she or he has access.

- **Don't compete with the computer.** Very few teachers can be more colorful or more engaging than a computer program or an email message from a friend. Design the computer lab in such a way that teachers can teach without interference from the computers. There are several ways to tackle this objective. One is to have the students turn around in their seats so that their backs are to the computers. Another option is to have the students turn off their monitors. You'll have to decide which system is most workable. The key thing to remember is that the computer is not an aide to teaching when you want the students' undivided attention. Another possibility is to use a remote control software program that will force every student computer to display what is on the instructor's computer. The instructor can release control when it's time for the students to do independent work. These remote-control programs also have the advantage of allowing the instructor to monitor what is on the screen of any computer in the lab.

- **Pay attention to the computer environment.** Little things that you might not notice with a single computer can be maddening when you have a roomful of them. Computers with noisy fans can make the lab feel like a day at the airport. The physical size of the computer and monitor affect the amount of space left for books and student papers. A few inches can be the difference between students working comfortably and having books and papers constantly falling to the floor.

- **Don't let lightning strike.** Lightning is a real danger in many parts of the world. One lightning strike can fry all of your computers, even if they are turned off. Almost as serious—and far more common—is the problem of poor electricity. Many schools were not designed with the modern equipment in mind. Telephones are rarities and classrooms may only have a few electrical outlets. Protect vulnerable computers with UPSes (Uninterrupted Power Supply). A UPS is essentially a battery with brains. It blocks surges and spikes—such as lightning—from reaching your equipment. It also adds power when the line voltage dips below a safe level—a power sag.

- **Seeing what you're doing.** Many computer labs are in former classrooms with wall-to-wall windows. The potential for glare is great. Glare is any reflection from an external light source on the computer's screen. When the glare is equal to or greater than the computer's image, the screen becomes difficult to see. Lower levels of glare wash out images and can cause eye strain. You can often avoid glare by correctly positioning the monitors—the correct way is the one where you don't see glare. Glare filters can help when there is no other option, but they don't solve every problem. One possibility is to put a shelf over the table with the monitors. If the shelf overhangs the monitors enough it may provide enough shade to block the glare. To determine a room's sources of glare, turn off the monitors and look at the reflections. What you see reflected on the blank monitor screen are sources of glare.
- **Chairs that roll.** If you have more than one student to a computer, they will most likely want turns at the keyboard. If you use the old fashion fixed-leg chairs, expect lots of scraping as students adjust their chairs. Swivel chairs are required if the students need to turn around to see the teacher.

It's a great idea to visit other school computer labs. Go during class periods to see how the design functions during use. All the principles mentioned here also apply to multimedia labs and to classrooms.

Library Computers

Computers destined for the library should probably be the same as the ones used in the computer lab. Remember, uniformity is a virtue when it comes to computers. If you, however, have some reasonable computers available from the old computer lab, the library may be a good place to put them. Students will most likely be doing word processing and Internet browsing. Naturally, the advice about glare and use of headphones also applies.

CD-ROM Towers

Libraries frequently use extensive collections of CD-ROMs. Having stacks of CD-ROMs next to each computer is not practical. CD-ROMs are easy to damage with normal handling—especially the "normal" handling of younger children. Leaving one on a hot radiator grill or on a sunny windowsill may be the last you'll see of the CD-ROM.

One of the most common solutions is to add a CD-ROM tower to the library network. These units are essentially music "jukeboxes" that play computer CD-ROMs. The user's computer sends a request over the computer network to the tower to use a specific CD-ROM. Because loading and playing the CD-ROMs can

Figure 11. CD-Rom Towers

be slow, many CD-ROM towers incorporate computer hard drives so that the tower can play from the hard disk rather than load, spinup, and read from the CD-ROM disk. The resulting speed improvement can be especially significant when several users want to use the same CD-ROM at the same time.

Hard drives have become so inexpensive that copying some or all of your CD-ROMs to the hard disk can be an economical solution. Just make sure the CD-ROM vendor either supports the copying of its CD-ROM to a hard disk or allows for it to be accessed over a network. Many vendors forbid one or both of these configurations because of fear of piracy.

Internet Filters

Internet filtering is perhaps the most contentious issue for school libraries. The issue is made even more difficult by the fact that the level of filtering for the library may need to be set differently than the filters for computers in other parts of the building. Here are some of the ways to implement filtering.

- **Filtering Services.** Some Internet service providers offer filtering as a service to their customers. AOL and MSN are two examples where "child-friendly" settings can be selected.
- **Filtering Software.** There are a number of software programs that monitor Internet use and block undesirable sites.
- **Site Restrictions.** Some browsers have the ability to check for special rating tags embedded in a website. Information about these tags can be obtained from the Internet Content Rating Association (www.icra.org). These tags can be used to identify a wide variety of content descriptors for one website or for one specific page. As the user, you can set your browsers to display pages with "fantasy violence" but not "sex." Websites that do have rating tags embedded in their pages don't display because the browser cannot assure that the site is safe. Unfortunately, this system is not in widely enough used to be a practical solution, but may come in handy if no other solution is available.

There are two main methods to determine appropriateness of a website. The first method is to filter incoming content as it comes into the system. The filter searches for targeted words and may even look for images that have a too much "flesh tones." The main problem with such a filter is that it can eliminate sites on sex education and breast cancer. If the filter is also looking for targeted words in email messages, it may not recognize "s*e*x" as being "sex." Porno spammers know the limits of common filters and design around them. As for scanning images, this is tricky at best. As flawed as content filters can be, schools have little choice but to consider them. The main advantage of such a system is that it may be able to block an unknown bad site.

The second method is based on using lists of "good" and "bad" sites. There are a number of firms that do nothing but label websites. The firm then sends out regular updates of the good and bad lists to their subscribers. The subscriber may add his or her own sites to the list.

A new area of concern is with search engines. Google can allow its users to see websites without having to actually visit the sites. This is done by using the "cache" option on the Google search result page. Google actually keeps copies of webpages on their site. Even after a website has been removed, Google may still be able to display its contents.

Images are another area of concern. For example, Google allows users to search for images without visiting the site from which the image resides. A student could enter a name of a famous person into a search engine's image search engine and come up with a listing of nude and seminude images. One protective measure you can take with Google is to turn on its built-in filter called SafeSearch. This setting offers protection against both "adult" images and text.

You don't have the time to look for all the ways around the filters—but the students do. Therefore, there is no substitute for simply watching the students. It's not hard to spot the commotion caused when a student stumbles across something he or she should not have found. You will hopefully be able to block the website in short order. You can also use computer-based logging programs to track student activity. If your students have found a way around the filter—and they probably will—the log files can show you this. Naturally, the age of the student and concerns for privacy must be weighed against the student's protection. The protection required for a high school student is different than that for a third grader.

Card Catalog Systems

Computerizing the old card catalog can transform many aspects of a library for the better, but it's a long and tedious process. The most common method is to enter the card catalog information into a database record and then link the book's record with a bar code strip affixed to the book. When the book is checked out, the barcode is scanned by an optical device. The computer tracks the book and the person who checked it out.

Any school just starting to look at computerizing the card catalog system should look at radio tags as an alternative to barcode strips. These radio tags—also known as "RFID"—are like super barcodes that can be scanned by simply walking by a radio-based scanner. Such a system would potentially allow students to walk past the reader with the books being automatically checked out. Librarians would be able to walk down the stacks with a reader to obtain a precise inventory of what is on the shelves. Inventories that might have been done on a yearly basis could literally be taken on a daily basis.

Administrative Offices

Security is the overriding requirement when planning computers for the school's administrative office. Whether the office is holding student records or the next pop quiz, the results from a security breach can be serious. The computers used by administrative staff need protection from both the Internet and from other computers in the school.

If you have any doubt about what you're doing in terms of security, disconnect any computers with very sensitive information from the local network and from the Internet. Isolating the computer and keeping it in a physically secure environment is the highest level of protection one can easily obtain. Unfortunately, much of the value of information comes from its sharing.

Internal Firewalls

Firewalls protect the "inside" from the "outside." Sometimes it makes sense to redefine parts of your school network as being inside and the other parts as being outside. Internal firewalls are not just about keeping students out of grades database; they can also provide another level of protection when a computer on the network becomes infected with spyware or a virus. The problem of spyware and viruses coming into the school has become more common as more students and staff take laptops home. While the laptop was away, the user probably did not have the same levels of protection afforded when they were at school.

PDAs (Personal Digital Assistants) are becoming attractive targets for virus writers and thus a security threat to the school's network. Users synchronize their PDAs with their work computer without any thought to potential security risks. As many mobile devices, including cell phones, become more like full-fledged computers, the opportunity for security problems increases. One new technology, Bluetooth, further increases the risk factor by creating a personal area network (PAN) that offers yet another route through which malicious programs can attack. Bluetooth does more than communicate; it can actively seek out other Bluetooth-enabled devices and establish connections without the user being aware. These connections are intended to be for the purpose of helping a PDA to synchronize with another one without requiring any technical proficiency of the user. Users may not know what Bluetooth is or understand the various security options included with Bluetooth. At this point, most of the viruses that have been targeted at PDAs have been relatively benign. However, given all the sensitive

Figure 12. VPN Tunnel

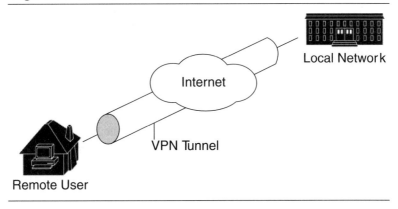

personal data that PDAs commonly contain and their ability to interact with computer networks, it is only a matter of time before more serious PDA-based security threats arrive.

With the price of firewalls constantly going down, using a few strategically placed units within the network can be a cost-effective means to increase security. There are a few factors to keep in mind when deploying an internal firewall. Most low-end firewalls are designed for the relatively slow speeds of an Internet connection. If a firewall is deployed within a local network, make sure the firewall is rated for the LAN's (local area network) connection speed.

There are some concerns that come with firewalls. For example, firewalls can cause communication problems with VPN (Virtual Private Network) connections. VPNs often require that they communicate directly. A firewall, especially if it uses a feature called Network Address Translation (NAT), may prevent the required direct connection. VPNs are often used by the school district's centralized accounting and student records systems. If your school has to use special computer links, make sure these links will not be adversely affected by the firewall. You may have to get a second line to the Internet for communicating with these systems.

Data Security

Student and staff records are so sensitive that extra security procedures should be considered. Here are a few possible ones.

- **Assure user identity.** Use a security card or token or some other physical device to unlock the computer. Not only are physical devices more secure than are passwords, but the computer automatically locks when the user removes the device. Some radio-based units can even detect when the user is more than a specified number of feet from the computer and subsequently locks the computer until the user returns. This protects against the situation where the computer operator runs out the room for an emergency and forgets to lock the computer.
- **Encrypt data.** Encrypt the sensitive storage areas on the disk so that an intruder cannot understand any information they might be able to copy. Encryption is a mathematical scrambling of data so that the data is unreadable to anyone without the code to unscramble it. Modern computers are so fast that this process does not significantly slow down the computer.
- **Lock down the hardware.** Physically secure the computer so that it won't be stolen. Consider locking the CPU case so that internal components cannot be removed. Some thieves will only take some of the computer's memory chips or some other component that might not be immediately noticed.
- **Lock away.** Consider using an external hard drive that can be locked in a safe at night.
- **Back up.** File backups can help you recover from a disk failure and are potentially useful when attempting to figure out when an intrusion took place. And, because most data is lost because of hardware failure or environmental causes, such as floods and lightning, a backup is critical to protecting your data.

Try to imagine how a possible abuser of your system might behave. Ask yourself how you would compromise the system if you were in their place.

Specialized Equipment

While you might have complete control over the elements of your design in the rest of the building, you may be forced by the school district to use certain equipment. For example, you may be required to call into the district mainframe computer via a modem to upload information. Below are some examples of specialized equipment that be may be found in a school administrative office.

- **Optical mark reader (OMR).** This is a scanner that reads the penciled-in circles on test-marking sheets.
- **Video surveillance system.** The addition of a computer to a video recording system can greatly help staff to find and analyze footage.
- **Employee time clock.** Using a computerized system to record employee hours greatly reduces the time required to consolidate information at the end of the week.
- **Computer-controlled door locks.** Controlling door locks by a computer can be ideal when a building is being used by a wide assortment of people and at all hours of the day. For example, you can provide an access card that opens some doors but not others and/or restricts access at certain times of the day. You can have a complete log of who opened which door. Plus, if you fire an employee, their access card can be deactivated instantly. You need not fear that keys were not returned or were inappropriately copied.
- **Automated calling system.** You can have a computer call a list of telephone numbers and leave variety of messages. You might want to remind parents of an upcoming meeting or notify them that their children are not in school. Not only does this relieve your staff of hours of routine calling, but it also gives you a record of your calls.

Movable Computer Carts

Computer labs on mobile carts are gaining popularity as laptop prices go down and wireless systems become more practical. The cart carries a wireless access unit that is hooked into the room's network port. These carts can be ideal for schools with classes with only periodic requirements for computers. For example, the history teacher sets aside a day for the students to research a study topic and does not want to have to schedule around the computer lab's availability.

There are a number of considerations specific to mobile carts. Here are a few to take into account.

- **Battery life.** Will the laptop batteries make it through the day or will extra batteries be required? How long does it take to charge an empty battery?
- **Wireless interference.** Does the school have sources of radio interference, such as microwave ovens, that could cause connection problems?

There are high-end wireless testers that can determine whether a location is good for wireless technology, but the best way to know is to get a wireless access point and a laptop with a wireless card. Buy the technology you plan on using with a 30-day return. If the hardware works, great. If not, return it and see if something else might work. Or see if you can determine the source of interference and remove it.

- **Security.** Can the units be physically secured to prevent theft? Theft can take place as the teacher rushes out the door and does not realize that one unit is not accounted for, or it can happen when someone breaks into the school at night and rolls the mobile cart right out the door.
- **Maintenance.** Can your plan handle the extra maintenance expense? Laptops are significantly more expensive than their desktop counterparts because parts are often specialized to the particular unit, and repairs frequently require a trip to the vendor. Laptops are also more likely to require repair than their desktop cousins because they are prone to being dropped.
- **Connection speed.** Do your students require high-speed connections? (*High speed* refers here to opening and saving multimedia files to the local server, not to high-speed Internet access.) Wireless connections are slower than wired connections. Certain types of work may not be practical if the last 10 minutes of the class is dedicated to saving large files over the wireless network to the school's file server.

Multimedia Centers

Multimedia centers get a great deal of attention because they are considered "sexy." They look impressive on paper and they excite the imagination. Excitement can be a blessing when you need to get funding for a new network. The downside is that high costs of multimedia projects can suck money from your basic services.

Multimedia computers can take as much power as you can afford. Video and audio work requires the computer to perform intensive calculations when creating transitional effects, such as applying filters or joining two video clips using a fade-in effect. Even a few videos can quickly chew up the largest hard disk. Video cards—normally not thought about much—need to be more powerful than the average. If you are planning to transfer video from a VHS tape or directly from a television, you'll need a video capture card.

Moving multimedia files requires fast network connections. This means 100 megabit connections to the desktops and preferably one-gigabit connections to the file server(s). Because of the strain large files can place on equipment and on the network capacity, you may want to consider segmenting your network. This means that all your media computers and file server(s) are connected to the same network switch. Traffic going between the multimedia computers and the server(s) do not need to traverse the school's general-purpose network. The only exception would be for Internet access.

As with all specialized designs, find the parts of the plan that are most constrictive and work around them. For example, review the video software for the specifications it requires. The last thing you want is to get an expensive computer only to find that the video card doesn't work with the software. Yet you may not need to be concerned with high performance if your work does not require it. Audio work is so much less demanding on the hardware that a less expensive computer can be purchased.

Video Cameras

If at all possible, get a digital video camera. Avoid the temptation to get a heavily discounted nondigital model. While the superior video-quality of a digital camera is a plus, the main reason to get a digital camera is the ease with which it works with today's video-editing software. If the video camera is fully supported by the editing software, you should be able to control the camera through the editing software. This allows you to watch the videotape or disk through the computer's monitor and only copy to the computer's hard drive those segments you want. With nondigital cameras, the entire video has to be imported to the computer's hard drive before the video software could view it. This transfer process, called *digitization*, requires large amounts of disk space and usually requires all the power your computer has.

For people very low on funds, the older predigital cameras work just fine, with the tradeoff that more time is necessary. With everyone upgrading to digital video cameras, perfectly fine nondigital video cameras can be obtained through donations. If the cameras are going to be used by young children or be exposed to possible breakage, you may feel more comfortable providing a less expensive camera. Just be aware that the main tradeoff is that it is more difficult to work with the resulting video than is true with digital cameras.

Buy a tripod for your camera. The number-one problem with most video shots is the constant moving and shaking of the person holding it. Anti-shaking features can smooth out some of the fine jiggling, but can do nothing for larger movements. A tripod also forces the user to think about the best camera position. People are so accustomed to the "natural" appearance of videos on TV that they assume that simply pointing the camera is enough. Few students know that what looks so easy on television is the result of multiple high-end cameras, professional editing, and multiple takes. All of which are, in brief, expensive.

A remote microphone is an inexpensive way to increase the quality of video dramatically. The position where one locates the camera is frequently not the ideal location for audio. Using the microphone in the camera also has the disadvantage of picking up the sound of the camera's various motorized components. People can tolerate shakiness or blurriness of the image, but distortions of the speaker's words are much less accepted. If your audience needs to understand the audio component, invest in an external microphone.

Scanners

Scanners are an absolute must for anyone working with graphics. Even for a multimedia lab completely dedicated to video, scanners can be used to insert photos and other graphics, such as charts and logos, into the video. The prices of scanners have come down so far that even a good scanner is affordable.

Scanners are deceptively simple. A few clicks of the mouse and the image appears on the screen. It's only later that the user finds out that all those settings that they didn't adjust can matter. For example, scanners frequently scan at a resolution of 300 DPI (dots per inch). This means that the image contains information for 300 dots for every square inch of the image. Because most laser printers use 300 DPI, images scanned for 300 DPI look great. The problem many users get into is that they use the settings for the printed page when creating an image intended for use on a website. A computer monitor displays 72 PPI (pixels per inch—same as DPI). PPI and DPI are the same type of measurement, but PPI applies to computer screens and DPI applies to printers. The problem is that computer monitors use 60–100 PPI and printers can print up to 1200+ DPIs. A file containing an image with 300 DPI worth of information has more than three times the required information. This extra information slows down the webpage with no benefit to the image's appearance. The extra information is simply extra baggage. With webpage sizes being extremely important to the speed of the website, a "heavy" scanned image can ruin the webpage's download performance.

The reverse problem is where an image is scanned in as a web image and printed on a laser printer. The result is a grainy image because the printer has only 1/3 of the information it needs to have. Many times you will want to use an image for multiple purposes. You can scan the image multiple times or you can scan the image in at the highest required setting and then use an image editor, such as Photoshop, to "optimize" the image for other display requirements.

VHS Players

Don't overlook the humble VHS player. A huge amount of content is still found in a VHS format. More importantly, VHS is a good presentation format because TVs with VHS players are easy to find. People can drive themselves crazy trying to figure out how to display video using computers and projectors when the solution is simply to put the video on a VHS tape.

Four-head units are a bit better than the less expensive two-head units when it comes to precise starting and stopping points on the tape. The additional two heads also allow for smooth slow-motion and clear images when the tape is stopped. Both of these features are important when it comes to precisely selecting video segments. If the frequent capturing of material from VHS tapes is anticipated, look for higher-end units that include sensitive tape position controls. While these features are nice, they are not essential. It's almost as easy to import slightly more than you need and prune away the extra in the video-editing program.

Sound Systems

As video quality has improved, sound has stayed pretty much the same. The problem is that most users use video cameras to capture sound. Look at a movie being shot and you'll see that the actors have microphones all around them, but there isn't one on the camera. The camera is often too far away to record good-quality sound. While a camera can zoom in on an image, the same cannot be done for the sound. To makes matters worse, the video's microphone is located next to the motor that auto-focuses the camera's lenses. For most purposes, sound is important and requires separate sound-recording equipment.

The key to good sound is to use the video camera's external microphone jack. The simplest method is to connect a microphone cable directly to the camera's jack. You can use either a microphone designed to be worn on the label or it can be a microphone designed for a microphone stand. Many users prefer wireless microphones because it allows them to move freely. This is more than just convenience; someone tripping over a microphone wire could result in the camera being toppled, and/or in personal injury. If you must lay a cable over a floor that gets lots of foot traffic, tape over the cables with gaffing tape, which will greatly lessen the chance of someone tripping and, unlike most other kinds of tape, will not damage most surfaces.

Not all microphones are created equal, or for the same purposes. Some microphones can cost more than the camera, and there is little chance you'll find a parent able to donate one of these. The key to saving money is to determine accurately what type of recordings you are likely to encounter. A low-quality microphone of the right type is better than a higher-quality unit intended for another purpose. If you can get only one microphone, the lavaliere type—for wearing on the lapel—is probably the most versatile. It works for mobile presenters, and can be attached to a podium as would a standard microphone. Its small size also gives it the advantage of not intimidating the user.

Camera operators tend to be very aware of the visual background when selecting a place to shoot, but few pay attention to the audio background of their filming location. Humans have the wonderful ability to tune out the cacophony of sounds that constantly bombard them. Sound systems don't have this ability. It's only later that you realize that your camera was next to an air-conditioner or that ambulances were passing by every five minutes. If you are able to pick the location of the shoot, listen carefully for hums, hisses, clicks, and other sounds that might drive your audience to distraction. A little attention to detail goes a long way. If you are planning on doing an important interview or special presentation, test the location by running a mock event. You'll be amazed by all the things you thought were working and don't, and by all the sounds and visual distractions you never noticed before.

As with a computer lab, consider providing your students with headsets so that speakers are not required. This alone can save the sanity of the media center teacher.

6

Network Infrastructure: Tying It All Together

Computers come and go, but wires are here to stay. Nothing in your network will last as long as its cabling. The quality of cabling affects the performance and stability of the network for years to come. If not installed properly, the wiring system could become a nightmare when higher-performance equipment is added to the network. Furthermore, network cabling problems tend to be some of the most difficult to identify and the costliest to repair. In short, do the job right the first time.

Design Considerations

If you have unlimited funds, install fiber optic cables to every device on the network. Fiber has virtually unlimited capacity, and its light-based system means that it is not affected by all the various forms of electromagnetic radiation found in every structure. But for those without unlimited funding, the design of a network is a series of trade-offs between cable distances, transmission speeds, reliability, and cost.

Distance

Some distances are fixed, such as the distance between two buildings, while other distances can be adjusted by rearranging equipment. All wireless and wired connections have distance constraints—even fiber-optic cables have meaningful distance constraints for those installing a transatlantic cable. For simplicity's sake, you only need to focus on a type of Ethernet cable called Category 5—also known as Cat 5 or Type 5 cable. This is the most common cable type used by network designers. Cat 5's ability to handle 10 and 100 Mbps (megabits per second) speeds makes it well suited for almost any desktop computer. Its distance limit of 100 meters (328 feet) can be extended by using any device, such as a router or switch, that amplifies the signal. Running a cable beyond its specified limit will result in the signal weakening through a process called "attenuation." Usually, the link degrades gradually as attenuation weakens the signal. At some point the signal will no longer be strong enough to be understood by the other side and the devices at both ends will give up.

In a computer lab, wiring distances are rarely an issue because of the short physical distances. Cable infrastructure design becomes more difficult, however, when it involves an entire building. If possible, the room where the main network switches are located should be centrally located to the majority of the connections within the building. For example, don't put your main network switches in the center of the building if 90% of your equipment is in the west wing and 10% is in the east wing. The objective is to get the lowest average run length with as few uncomfortably long runs as possible.

Servers and switches are normally located in the same room. While less convenient, there can be good reasons why the two systems may be separated. One such reason would be if your building has a small closet in one part of the building that is perfect for the wiring design but not large enough to handle the file servers. In this case, you put the switches into the closet and install a fast connection, perhaps fiber optic, between the main switches and the server room. It's easier if all your central equipment is in one physical location, but not mandatory.

While no single Cat 5 cable can go more than 100 meters, the total distance can be extended as long as there is another switch or router to amplify the signal. It is common in large buildings to connect all the cables on one floor to its own wiring closet. The wiring closets on each floor are then connected together to the main wiring closet. The connection that vertically connects all the wiring closets is often called the *riser* or *backbone*. This arrangement is typical in multistoried buildings.

Wireless technology has become an important factor when designing a network. Wireless technology may be the only way to solve certain problems, such as providing connectivity to students sitting outdoors. Yet it is risky to design a network completely based on wireless technology. Wireless connections are prone to environmental factors.

The problem with wireless connectivity is that there is no guarantee of reception distances and connection speeds. You cannot simply draw a circle around each wireless access point and assume every computer will enjoy the connection speed listed on the box. First of all, wireless access points functions like hubs. That means that the users share bandwidth. Each new user further divides the same pie. Connection speeds are also adversely affected as distance increases. Usually there is a linear progression between distance and the lowering of the connection speed on a wireless connection, but environmental factors such as walls and trees can have a dramatic effect. Even in an open area, wireless access points are not always consistent. Some access points may have worse connections when the distance is less than 1 foot than they do at 10 feet. Some access points use directional antennas, thus making the connections in front of the antenna better than those behind it.

There are a frustratingly large number interference factors that can further decrease wireless performance. Microwave ovens and cordless phones may share the same wireless transmission frequencies. Other wireless devices can conflict with your device. An especially difficult situation is where two wireless access points are equally distant from a user. The devices may actually fight over which device supplies service to the user. If the user is moving around the room, the constant tug-of-war between the two devices can produce horrible results. Corporations frequently use master controllers to control all the access points so that users are gracefully moved from one device to another. Unfortunately, in the world of education, these systems are really only affordable for universities and very well-financed schools.

Building structure also plays a part. Brick and cement walls are less friendly to wireless transmissions than are drywall or plaster. The best way to know if something will work is to test it in the situation in which you intend to use it.

Connections can be improved by careful placement of access points, the addition of antenna boosters, and the appropriate selection of communication settings. Many access points can be found on a desk in the corner of a room. This is a great location if you want to provide wireless access to the street outside, but poorly uses the access point's coverage area. The access point would probably work best if it could be mounted on the ceiling in the middle of the coverage area rather than being located in the corner.

Having more access points is not always better when it comes to providing complete coverage. Access points can interfere with each other. So, rather than place a wireless point in every classroom, you might get better performance if the access point was mounted in the hallway between classrooms. When the building's use of construction materials limits access points within the building, explore the option of placing the access point on the outside of the building. No matter how solid your school's walls might be, the school probably has windows on most of its rooms. Placing a few access points on poles facing the building's windows is a good way to avoid nasty internal issues. It can also provide you with the start of an external network.

Cable Types

There are many types and shapes of cables. The average school technician only needs to know about a few wire types. Below is a list of common Ethernet cable types and their characteristics.

- **Category 3:** Designed for telephone use, these cables are very limited when used for computer networks. While you can live with it when already installed, you should not install any more of it—even for telephone service. Use the better Cat 5 cable so that you have the option of using it for computer connections at some future point.
- **Category 5:** Cat 5 is the workhorse of network cabling. Still a good choice for connecting desktop computers.
- **Category 5e:** The *e* stands for *enhanced*. This gives you confidence that you'll get the most out of high-speed connections. Consider this for connecting servers, switches, and multimedia desktop computers. The price difference between Cat 5 and Cat 5e in terms of price is low enough to pick Cat 5e in most situations.
- **Fiber Optic:** Fiber optic is good for connecting buildings on a campus. It can be used for connecting very powerful servers with gigabit-speed switches. They also can come in handy if network cabling has to pass through any extreme form of electrical interference.

Installation

When is a Cat 5 cable *not* a Cat 5 cable? When it is installed incorrectly. Cable category specifications include how the cable is to be installed. Many people ignore the specifications only to wonder why their cable is not performing correctly. Here are a few of the "don'ts" of Cat 5 cable installation. Most of these common-sense rules apply to most forms of cabling—fiber optic has its own rules.

The *don'ts* . . .

- Bending the cable more than 90 degrees. A common mistake when a cable is stapled along the wall.
- Allowing the cable to coil or loop can produce radio interference. Cables, except for the fiber-optic kind, produce radio waves. When the cable is coiled, the signal from one part of the cable can interfere with the signal from another part of the cable.
- Running a cable over fluorescent-light ballasts can result in interference.
- Removing extra insulation from the cable ends when attaching the connectors.
- Kinking or snagging the cable. A kink can weaken the cooper inside the cable and reduce its signal strength.
- Staples can puncture and pinch the cable. Even when the staple does not penetrate the cable's casing, the force of a staple gun can still crush the cable against the wall.
- Yanking or pulling hard on a cable can damage it. Cables should not be under tension after being installed. Be especially aware of pulling the cable over a sharp edge. You'll be amazed at how many sharp edges there are inside ceilings and walls. It's very tempting to want to pull a stuck cable as you're pulling it through the wall or ceiling.
- Walking on the cable can damage it.
- Cables should not share conduit with electrical wires.

Fire codes also play an important role. In most localities, cables that run through enclosed spaces, such as ceilings and walls, need to have a plenum coating. This coating increases the cable fire rating. Cables that are in the open may use the less expensive PVC coating.

If you are going to do your own wiring, you will need to learn how to terminate the cable ends, either with a plug or by using a wall port. Your first attempts will be full of failures. Leave yourself some extra cable length on your first few attempts. Better yet, practice a few times on spare cable before doing it for real. After the first few connections, the task becomes easier. You will need plugs and/or ports, a *crimper* (a pliers-like device that forces the plug to grab the loose wires), and a line tester. Line testers can cost thousands of dollars, but a $40 dollar one is usually enough. The expensive testers will tell you what's wrong and where, while the cheap testers will only tell you to try again.

Most people will opt to use professional cable installers. If your building is unionized, you probably have no choice. If your installation requires substantial work above ceilings and in the walls, professional installers should be used. Working above the ceiling can be quite dangerous. There are many sharp edges, and falling through is always a real possibility. Dropped or suspended ceilings are designed to handle the weight of ceiling and not 200-pound weekend warriors.

The primary tool for pulling cables is a coiled ribbon of metal called a *snake*. The snake is used by first pushing and sliding the snake from where you want the cable to go to where the cable current is located. The cable is then attached to the end of the snake. Often the snake will have a loop or hook the cable can be attached to. If all goes well, pulling the snake back will bring the cable with it. In a long run, the cable may need to be snaked a few times using intermediary points.

Snakes should be treated with caution because they have a tendency to whip back at the user.

Another advantage to using a professional installer is that they will have expensive cable testers. Make it a condition of the contract that every line will be tested either in your presence or with a paper printout. Any cable that cannot pass the tester must be replaced with a new cable. This is especially important if your cable will be expected to operate at close to its rated speed. A cable can have a problem that will allow it to function at low speeds but not at higher speeds.

Over-Build to Have Enough

There is a Scottish saying: Leave early to arrive on time. The networking corollary is to build more than you need in order to have enough. One common error that network designers make is to run cables to every place where a connection is required at that point in time. Human nature being what it is, the day after finishing a new cabling system users will want to move desks or add computers. Perhaps the teacher's lounge will be converted to a computer lab or the school district will ask that IP telephones be added to the school's network. While you cannot prepare for every possibility, you should prepare for likelihoods.

Running extra cables does not significantly increase the cost. The main expense with installation is the manpower involved. Pulling wires can be time-intensive. Because the price of the cabling is fairly reasonable when purchased in bulk, pulling two cables instead of one is not that much more expensive. In fact, some organizations pull fiber-optic cables with their regular cables just in case they want to use them at some point. This is called running "dark" cable. In contrast, running a cable after the installation has been completed is usually very expensive. There's no bulk discount on the wire, holes have to be made in the ceiling and walls, labor costs will be at their maximum, and there is even a good chance that the dragging of the new wire will accidentally snag an old cable and thus damage it.

It's good practice to run extra cables for important connections—such as the connection between the computer lab and the main wiring closet. If the first cable fails, you can switch to the second cable. Installing extra cables does not mean you have to purchase more hubs and switches. Leave the unused cables unconnected until needed. If someone moves a desk, simply move the connection to the switch from the old location to the new location. Higher-end servers often come with a second connection for use as a backup to the primary connection. It is also possible for the second cable to be "bridged" with the first cable so that there is now twice the bandwidth.

Patch Panels

A patch panel is one item that's easily overlooked when listing network components. It is a connector board where network cables running to the wiring closet can be terminated. The panel is like a massive wall jack. Panels have ports for every cable that comes to the wiring closet. Patch panels are not expensive, but they certainly can look daunting to install. Hiring a professional installer makes sense.

Figure 13. Front of Patch Panel

Figure 14. Back of Patch Panel

Technically it is possible to do without a patch panel and terminate each cable with a plug but this tends to result in a wiring mess. Most networks have more cables than are used at any given time. The patch panel provides a clean way to handle the unused cables because they can be terminated to the back of the patch panel rather than left dangling.

Another advantage to patch panels is that they usually have space on the front panel for identifying the cable. Labeling your cables saves a tremendous amount of time when you are tracking down a network problem. The optimal system is to write some sort of code on the panel and on the connector plate in the user's office. Don't label the cable after a person—for example, "Carl's office." It's unlikely that Carl will still be in that office 20 years later. If possible, try to organize the cables on the patch panel so that physical locations are grouped together. For example, each floor can have its own row on the panel, or one row could be just for the computer lab. Taking time to organize and label your cables will really pay off.

Hubs and Switches

Hubs and switches can be thought of as a network's heart in that they circulate data from place to place. While a hub broadcasts data to all users, a switch forwards incoming data to an addressed user. Hubs are appropriate for situations where you need to share a single connection between two computers, but for most other purposes, use a switch. Switches are faster and they provide better security because one user does not have the ability to see the data that is addressed to other users. Switches also have the ability to isolate a troublesome network connection before the entire network is affected. The extra features of a switch are normally well worth the extra cost.

Both hubs and switches are simple to set up. In general, just plug in the cables and turn them on. Expect hubs or switches to function for many years without a problem.

7

Dealing with Vendors

Computers may be complicated and frustrating to the average person, but they may be a euphoric experience for your vendor. Understanding vendor characteristics and motivations are important to obtaining the right equipment.

Vendor Bias

Most sane people go home at the end of the day and do something completely unrelated to their jobs. But computer geeks go home, turn on their home computer networks, and start "playing" with new programs and new equipment. While this emotional attachment can be a good thing, it can also produce strong biases. A strong bias is like a misaligned gun sight. If you can compensate for the bias, the aim may still be fairly accurate. It's not knowing about a bias that makes hitting the mark difficult.

Computer vendors tend to have strong beliefs about technology, especially when discussing computer operating systems (Windows vs. Linux vs. OS X), computer hardware (PCs vs. Macs and Intel vs. AMD), and between Open Source software and proprietary software. Every vendor has an opinion. The key for you is to find a vendor whose bias is not so strong that it will cause an obvious solution to be overlooked.

Ask questions of all prospective vendors. You don't need to master the subject matter to hear the sharp edge of a fanatical view. You should expect reasoned answers rather than grand pronouncements. If you hear statements like "xyz is garbage" or "it's immoral to use abc," run away. Even a statement such as "we only use xyz" may be a warning. A strongly biased vendor certainly isn't going to be proposing a solution that includes some technology that they hate passionately.

Bidding

If you are purchasing only a few computers, you can research prices on the Internet. Large purchases, however, should go through a bidding process. A bidding process often entails inviting three vendors to submit proposals. Look around to see which vendors can do the type of work you require, and check references and the Better Business Bureau to assure that you're only dealing with reputable vendors.

A bidding process usually starts with a RFP (Request For Proposal). A RFP describes in a fair amount of detail what you expect in the vendor's proposal. The accuracy and clarity of your RFP will greatly impact the quality of the bids you receive.

On the one hand, vague statements such as "We want a schoolwide computer network" will result in so much variation between bids as to make comparison next to impossible. On the other hand, specifying specific equipment may lock the vendor into offering you what you asked for and not what is best for your needs. So, be specific as to *what* you want accomplished and be less specific about *how* it has to be accomplished. Make it clear in your RFP that the bids are final. Some vendors employ a technique of providing a profit-laden bid with the expectation that they will be able to "match or beat" any bid that comes in lower. That's not fair to the other vendors and it encourages everyone to give you a padded bid. Tell them that bids are final—and mean it. Your school has a reputation to protect, just as much as they do.

Monetary gain is another form of bias that you need to be alerted to. This bias is not so easy to identify because the vendor does not have a belief system surrounding it. If a vendor is an authorized reseller for a certain manufacturer, don't be surprised if the proposal exclusively uses equipment from that manufacturer. Even if the vendor can sell you equipment from another manufacturer, the profit margins will most likely differ. In fact, your order of 50 recently discontinued computers may be just what the vendor needs to get a free vacation or a bonus from the manufacturer. Rewards and profitability are legitimate interests of the vendor, but it becomes your concern when the vendor wants to sell you computers that may not serve your best interests.

In most cases, vendors anticipate making most of their profits from service and support. Hardware is rarely profitable to the seller. The real money is in servicing what you've been sold. If you plan to use a vendor for service, let them know. They may be willing to lower the price on the hardware to get your business.

Consultants

Consultants can help cut through the jungle of details and competing claims. A good consultant should be a good listener and able to communicate ideas without techno-babble.

As with vendors, you need to determine whether there are any significant biases. You should also check to make sure that the consultant is not a vendor or working with a vendor. Vendor relationships can compromise the quality of the advice you're given. Check references to see how past projects have turned out. The consultant should have experience with your particular situation. Consultants with only high-end corporate experience have a tendency to recommend solutions that only corporations with deep pockets can afford. They also have a hard time envisioning how computer equipment is used—and abused—in the school environment. Some high-end consultants may simply be unwilling to adjust their advice even when they do understand your requirements. Some simply don't know the nonpremium manufacturers. Similarly, there is a risk factor associated with using less-expensive equipment. The equipment may not be as good and the support may not be as complete. The consultant could look bad if the system disappoints in any way. It's all very understandable, but when you require someone to help you squeeze the last penny out of the proposal, you may find that the consultant is unable to help you.

Make it clear to a consultant from the start what you expect and how long you are interested in using his or her services. Consultants have a natural interest in getting more billable hours. Tasks that were never considered before are added. Jobs that you had planned on doing in-house become more easily done by the consultant. It's not uncommon that the consultant could very well become a de facto permanent employee whose original mandate has long been forgotten but whose hourly rate lives on. That's not to say that asking a consultant with whom you are pleased to stay longer is wrong; just be conscious of your decisions and its impact on the budget.

Saving Money

Schools and nonprofits are often eligible for discounts. Discounts for hardware tend to be fairly small given their already small margins, but software can be discounted by 50% or more. In some situations, outright donations are possible. If you aren't aware of these discounts and use the local vendor, you may end up paying far more than necessary.

Call up software vendors and ask them what their policy is for educational discounts. Each vendor's policy is different. Another way to potentially save on software is to consider a site license. A site license is an agreement with the software vendor that your organization may use its software on any computer within the organization. As with discounts, site licenses vary in many ways. Make sure you understand the details.

The best deals on hardware are often obtained by purchasing "refurbished" units, or equipment that has been sent back to the vendor and repaired. More often than not, a refurbished unit may have been returned still in the box due to the buyer's inability to pay or because the order was inaccurate. For all practical purposes, refurbished units are just as good as new units and the discount can be significant.

Saving money doesn't have to end with products. There are many nonprofit organizations staffed by volunteer computer professionals with the goal of helping schools and nonprofits with computer services. A quick search on the Internet will usually find a local volunteer organization. Even if one is not local, you can still get help from one via telephone and email. You cannot expect the same level of responsiveness to your needs as you would expect from a paid consultant, however. If nothing else, a volunteer consultant can help you frame the questions before looking for a professional consultant. Another advantage to a volunteer consultant is that they will certainly understand that you need to operate within a tight budget.

Before pulling out your wallet, see if there are any technology grants for which you may be eligible. Funding organizations is like making grants for technology. It doesn't hurt to call some of the local politicians and service organizations to see if they know of any sources of help.

Don't forget sweat-equity. There is a lot a quickly trained individual can do. For example, they can run cables along walls and set up new computers. After installation, you can use them to run the auto-updating systems on each computer. Activities like this are not hard to do but do take a long time. If a vendor charges you for these routine services, your total bill will be much higher. So buy the computers from a vendor, have them do the difficult work, and then have your local volunteers do the routine work. Even something as simple as having your volunteers unpack all the new computers and connect the wires can save hours of very expensive time. Volunteers can be staff, parents, or students.

8

Multi-Function vs. Single-Function Servers

The age-old debate of whether to use a general-purpose tool or a single-purpose tool is alive and well in the computer age. There are compelling arguments on both sides. The size of the organization and the nature of the task are just two important considerations.

Multi-Function Servers

A *multi-function server* can be defined as one that runs two or more important services. Some examples of important services include file server, email server, firewall, web server, print server, proxy server, and directory server. Supporters of the multi-function server philosophy argue that putting several services on a single computer can make technical and economic sense. Here are a few arguments in favor of a multi-functional server.

- **Quality over quantity:** Placing multiple services on one computer allows you to buy a better server than you would if you had split your budget between several less powerful computer servers.
- **Cost savings:** A single powerful computer may cost less than the purchase of several less powerful units. You may also save money on software costs since you require fewer copies.
- **Tighter integration:** Some systems, such those from Microsoft, often integrate more easily if they are installed on the same computer. When services are separated, the network administrator may have to enter user information multiple times. Not only is this time-consuming, but typos can create problems down the line.
- **Consolidation:** Backing up the server is easier when all the services are on one physical device.
- **Space and energy savings:** A single server will take up less physical space and require less electricity than will a group of servers. This is an especially important factor for schools, because they often have poor electrical and air-conditioning services.

Single-Function Servers

Supporters of single-function servers and their cousins, network appliances, have a very different philosophy from that of the multi-function server supporters.

The core principle is that complexity is the enemy of reliability. A single-function system can be optimized in ways that a multi-function server cannot be. Here are some supporting arguments.

- **Simplicity:** Single-function servers are less likely to fail because they do not have to interact with other services on the same computer.
- **Isolation:** A security breach of one service does not expose other services. Similarly, runaway processes or unexpected levels of data storage won't adversely affect other services because they have their own processors and hard drives. To use an extreme example, a service may cause the computer to crash or lock up, but services on other computers will continue to function.
- **Hardware reuse:** Multiple lower-end computers have the potential to be less expensive than a big multi-function server because you might be able to reuse older computers that would otherwise not have a purpose.
- **Minimization of finger pointing:** One of the main problems with obtaining support on a multi-function server is that the technical support technicians will have a tendency to blame other services—the proverbial finger-pointing game. It's easier to assign responsibility if each service runs on a dedicated computer. The exception to this rule is where a multifunctional computer is running software from a single vendor.
- **Fall-over hardware:** A single-function computer can be used to replace the service on another computer in case of failure. Let's say the web server computer dies—the web server software could be temporarily installed on the email server and activated in cases of emergency. You can even have the software installed on multiple computers just so you can quickly switch. In fact, it is entirely possible to have your servers monitor the health of the other computers and turn of services when a unit dies or is otherwise not functioning. While it is possible to do this with multifunctional servers, their expense makes a similar backup plan financially out of reach for most schools.

Finding a Balance

There is no one right answer regarding which philosophy works best. For a small, low-budget, network, leaning toward single-function servers may make sense. The chance that your entire network will be brought down is reduced. The redundancy factor of a multi-functional server with a hot backup server is often not possible. Putting in an expensive "backup server" is a tough sell to a nontechnical administrator. They'll cross it out as proof to their bosses that they did their best to save money. Naturally, they'll not remember this when the entire network is down.

The balance is not black-and-white, or a formula that can be used to plug in variables. Here are a few of the questions you need to ask.

- What combination reduces costs the most?
- Do some services benefit from being on the same computer?

- Will the addition of another service to a computer adversely affect performance and/or reliability?
- Are the services separate from, or dependant on, one another? For example, email and file serving are separate, but the web server and its supporting database server are codependant. Things that are dependant can be on the same computer, but things that are separate probably should not be. If the email server brings down the computer, you don't want your users to also be without the file server.

Sometimes the solution is to outsource or eliminate the need for a server. In the case of email, small schools should consider using an external email service provider. This may cost a bit more, but it has the potential to save your school's Internet bandwidth because external email providers often offer antivirus and anti-spam services. Spam and viruses generally represent between 50 and 80% of all messages. If you run your own email server, all those undesirable messages have to come over your Internet connection. Web serving is one of the other common services that is outsourced.

In some cases, the best solution to is to eliminate the server. Printer servers can now be replaced with networked printers, where users print directly to the printers over the local area network. In fact, it is possible with many of the newer printers to print to them over the Internet. There are situations in which the traditional system of sending all the print jobs to a centralized printer server has advantages. For example, a print server can allow for better centralized administration. It can help if you want to balance the load amongst a group of printers or you want to charge users for the pages they print. Naturally, the downside to a centralized printer server is a single point of failure. Setting up the network so that users print directly to networked printers avoids this problem of a single point of failure. As long as the users can find one working printer on the network, they should be able to print.

One tip on saving money with network printers is to buy the network interface separately. Printer vendors frequently charge exorbitant amounts for the network connection for the printer. They know that anyone buying a printer that costs over 1,000 dollars is probably going to be installing it on a network. That allows them to make the price of the "optional" network card multiples of what it should be. As an alternative, you can purchase an inexpensive external print server and connect it to the printer through a parallel or USB cable.

9

Security Overview

Security must be considered during the design phase. Too many security plans are jury-rigged after a security breach. Security in the Internet age has to be a constant concern. When your school connects to the Internet, it is in effect opening its doors to every person on the Internet. Hackers in Estonia, pornographers in Japan, scam artists in Nigeria, and terrorists in Pakistan are now the school's next-door neighbors. While the Internet creates a bevy of new threats, the greatest threat comes from insiders.[4] The modern computer network is a powerful tool, and you can count on it being used against you.

It's not difficult to protect your school from 90% of security problems. Of the remaining 10%, half can be handled by more advanced techniques, and the remaining half is luck. The hard reality is that there is no guarantee a determined and skilled adversary can be kept out. If you discover that your network has been compromised by a hacker, the best course of action is to cut the affected unit's network connection and rebuild it from a freshly formatted drive.

Risk Assessment

The most important step you can take in the protection of your school is to correctly assess your most likely threats. Risk assessments help you to determine what you need to protect. While it may be appealing to think that one can protect against all types of threats, it is sobering to remember that even the Great Wall of China didn't prevent invasion. The key is to build a security wall around your valuable assets that is "high enough" to discourage a would-be attacker. Attempting to build the electronic version of the Great Wall wastes money and may result in a wall that is not high enough at the right place to protect against a specific attacker. Risk assessment requires that three questions be answered:

1. What does your school have of value?
2. Who would want these valuables?
3. How much effort and money would an attacker be willing to expend to get these valuables?

---

4. *CSI/FBI Computer Crime and Security Survey*, by L. A. Gordon, M. P. Loeb, W. Lucyshyn, & R. Richardson. Computer Security Institute Publications, 2005, p. 15.

Stating that you want to protect your "property" or "computer data" is not specific enough. Clearly, your student records and vendor account information are far more valuable than are fliers advertising your next fund-raiser. Being specific about what you consider valuable will greatly help you in designing an effective protection plan.

There are numerous forms of attacks and almost as many motivations behind them. Most attacks will not be directed against your school specifically. In fact, most electronic attacks are designed to systematically attack everyone. Many attacks are the result of young men and women wanting to see if they can launch a successful attack, but an increasing number of attacks are from organized crime syndicates. These criminals want to obtain credit card and identification information.

Fortunately, most security attacks are opportunistic in nature. In other words, the attacker is looking for an easy victim and will bypass anyone sufficiently protected. The goal, therefore, is to be better protected than those around you. Given the general population's abysmal level of computer security, this is not difficult to do.

As odd as it might seem, more security is not always best. Extremely high levels of security can impinge on your network's ability to function. It may also create so much confusion that users bypass security steps. Once again, it is vital to know what and against whom you're protecting yourself. As a bridge engineer once said, the trick is not to build a bridge that is strong enough; it's to build a bridge that is *just* strong enough.

Patches and Fixes

Most security attacks take advantage of vulnerabilities that have long been recognized and fixed. The problem is that most users are unaware of the vulnerabilities and the relevant patches and fixes. Virtually all software will have serious vulnerabilities at some point in time. It's not a question of *if*, but of *when*. Owning a piece of software requires that you check for fixes. Just as no one buys a car without expecting to change the oil, no one should expect the purchase of a software program to be the end of the story.

While the operating system is the most important piece of software to keep updated, don't forget the applications that run on the operating system. Hackers are starting to attack the applications more often because they know that users are not updating them with the same frequency as the operating system. On a user's computer, the applications they may attack could be the email client or the web browser. On a server, it may be the email server or the application running the website. One of the newest targets for hackers is the backup system. The backup system is often installed and forgotten. Yet it has all the most important data in one place. Simply put: Hackers adapt, and so must you.

The best way to find out about security problems is on the software vendor's website. Lesser-known products may require a check every few months, while better-known products, like Microsoft Windows, should be checked on a regular basis—in particular, the second Wednesday of the month, because Microsoft now releases new security patches on the second Tuesday of each month. Many software programs allow you to check automatically for updates over the Internet. The updates with which you should be most concerned are those labeled "security" and/or "critical." Other updates may only be new product features that you may or may not be interested in.

While Microsoft products are the ones that get the most press in terms of security patches, all operating systems require patching. Computer experts love to debate which operating systems are most secure, but the key factor is the knowledge of its user. Even the most secure operating system is in danger if the person in charge of it doesn't understand it.

Encryption

Encryption is a word that many people recognize, few understand, and even fewer know how and when to use. It is the scrambling of information so that it can only be read by authorized individuals. There are two parts to any form of encryption: the computer code that decides how to scramble the information, called the *algorithm*, and the password, called the *key*. Both parts need to be "strong" for the encoded information to be secure. The most secure program is useless if the password is easily determined; likewise, the best password offers little protection when the encryption program is weak.

Encryption is used in many places and with varying levels of security. On the Internet, people use encryption all the time without even knowing it. For example, when you see the symbol of a lock on your browser bar during an online purchase, that symbol indicates that all the communication between you and the remote web server is encrypted. The system does not need to ask you for a password because your browser and the web server that you are connecting to automatically create and exchange passwords in a process called a key exchange.

Encryption should always be used when sensitive information, such as your login information, is passed over the Internet (this includes web-based email systems, uploading web content to remote web servers, and secured websites). Encryption of documents sent by email is another valid use and should be considered when highly sensitive information is being sent. It is also a virtual requirement for laptops holding sensitive documents. Encrypting documents or even the entire hard drive makes it far more difficult for a thief to browse the contents. The thief would have to know the username and password to read the documents. Fortunately, the newer operating systems

Figure 15. Encyrption Process

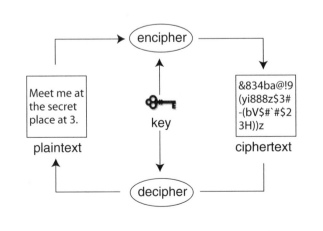

allow the user to encrypt entire directories and folders automatically on the hard disk. The user doesn't even notice the encryption because the files are automatically encrypted and decrypted by the operating system.

Before you go out and encrypt everything possible, however, it is important to know some of the dangers of encryption. First, if one of your users encrypts his or her information and then forgets the password or suddenly leaves, all the encrypted information will most likely be permanently inaccessible. It may make sense to have your users place their passwords in sealed envelopes that can be stored in a very safe place, such as a safe deposit box. The second problem is that of password management. A lock isn't very good if everyone has a key. While sending encrypted documents between two people isn't difficult, things get more difficult when you send to groups. Getting the password to them all in such a way that the password is not compromised is possible but tedious.

One of the most serious dangers of encryption is that it can create a false sense of security. When someone encrypts a document, for instance, the unencrypted version of the document may still exist. Computer operating systems and word processors have a number of features operating in the background to protect the user from losing data. These protective measures are great when your computer suddenly crashes and you get a restored backup file when the computer comes back up, but may introduce all types of vulnerabilities when you're attempting to control information. No level of protection can avoid the fact that you need to type and read the document in unencrypted form. Key loggers (i.e., programs that record the user's keystrokes surreptitiously) and spyware that takes photos of the screen are obviously serious threats to even the best protected file.

Strong Passwords

Passwords, especially on publicly accessible systems, are vulnerable to a variety of automated password attacks. Attackers, for example, can feed in all the words found in a dictionary against the password system. A surprising number of passwords can be found this way. Another method of attack is to run through combinations of letters and numbers until the right combination has been reached. This method works well for passwords of four or less characters but becomes impractical when six or more characters are used in the password.

A strong password has the following three characteristics:

* Not found in any dictionary.
* More than six characters in length. Every additional character vastly increases the difficulty for password-cracking programs.
* The password should not be guessable. Avoid using a password that can be easily associated with you or your school.

According to these rules, "xX897ab%Y17!!!8eF" may appear to be an excellent password, but it may be too difficult for the user to remember. Frequently such hard-to-remember passwords are written down on a post-it note and affixed to an obvious location. The result is a password that isn't secret.

It makes sense to create passwords from combined letters and numbers that have meaning to the user and thus are easy for that user to remember. So, the name and age of your mother's dog could be good: *Rover6*. An old address would work: *15BakerAve*. Note the use of upper and lower case letters. Many computer systems distinguish between "A" and "a." By using a combination of upper- and lower-case characters, you make the password cracker's job vastly more difficult.

The strongest password isn't much protection if an attacker can easily obtain it. Many programs for transferring files over the Internet, for example, send the password "in the clear." In other words, the password is readable by anyone able to capture the login process. As a rule, never send passwords across the Internet in the clear. It's not always obvious when a password is being sent in the clear. Telnet and FTP programs always send in the clear. Many web design programs upload files via FTP, so they are sending in the clear as well. If you are logging in via an Internet browser, look for the lock symbol on the status bar (seen at the bottom of the screen). If you do not see the lock, you may be sending in the clear. Free, secured communication programs, such as PuTTY,[5] are essential for any type of Internet connection where a username and password is used. This software creates an encrypted connection before the username and password are transferred. Anyone capturing such a connection will find the data completely scrammed and unusable.

Just as an overly complex password encourages the user to write it down, having too many passwords produces the same result. Because it is impractical to have users remember dozens of different passwords, they should consolidate their passwords to a manageable number. For example, use one password for unimportant Internet sites while having another for important Internet sites (such as bank accounts and places where private information is kept). Do the same thing within your network: one password for your regular login and another one for administrative tasks.

Hardening the Operating System

Hardening is the process by which an operating system or software application is made more difficult to attack. Even operating systems such as Microsoft Windows can be hardened. Generally, most of the steps involve turning off extraneous services. Computer vendors tend to ship their operating systems with everything turned on by default. This is done so that the user does not get the mistaken impression that the operating system is somehow broken or otherwise limited. Unfortunately, these unnecessary services can become points of vulnerability for hackers. In many cases, the user does not even know that a service in need of patching is actually installed and running. This is one important reason why a knowledgeable user is vital to the overall security of the system.

Hardening is especially important for servers exposed to the public, such as web and email servers. To find out how to harden your operating system, go to a standard Internet search engine, such as Google, and type in the name of your operating system and the term *harden* or *hardening*. Remember that after every upgrade, you may have to redo the process.

---

5. PuTTY: A Free Telnet/SSH Client. Available at http://www.putty.nl

Defense in Depth

Defense in depth means that your security measures employ multiple layers of protection due to the fact that one layer will probably have a security hole in it at some point in time. The fluid nature of what is and isn't secure requires that second-level and third-level forms of protection be in place when the first level of protection fails. Don't put all your eggs in one basket.

Although constantly updating a software program protects against attacks that are known, occasionally attacks take advantage of security vulnerabilities that are unknown or have yet to be fixed—called *zero day exploits* because the exploit came before a warning could be given. Most operating systems and Internet web browsers consistently have a list of known problems that have yet to be addressed. What's on the list may change, but the fact that items are always on the list does not change. Given this reality, you need to employ other forms of protection, such as firewalls, to block the attacker's access to these security vulnerabilities. Think of each layer of protection as being like a window screen. All the little holes represent vulnerabilities. If multiple layers of the screen are overlapped, the screens now function as a solid wall.

10

Viruses and Spyware

Viruses are one of most significant security threats your school will face. Spyware is one of the newest and fastest-growing security threats. In some cases it is difficult to decide which is which because they often share features. In both cases, someone has written computer code to use someone else's computer to do things the owner does not want to have done.

Viruses

A computer virus is simply a malicious program, or *malware* (malicious-logic software), designed to attach itself to other programs and replicate. There are three main types of malicious programs:

- Trojan horse (includes spyware)
- Worm
- Virus

Although all malicious programs have properties in common, namely, that they are designed for the purpose of doing something bad and/or unauthorized, they may act differently or have different objectives. Even within a category type, there is great variation.

Virus writers and antivirus vendors are in a constant battle with each other to gain the upper hand. While there are thousands of viruses roaming the world's computer systems, it is the newest viruses with which you have to be most concerned. Before the Internet, a new virus took a long time to circulate. Most of the older viruses required the user of the infected computer to copy some file to a floppy disk that would then be given to another user. The time between infection of the first victim and the second victim could be days, weeks, or months. The Internet has transformed the environment so that the first infected computer instantly starts to infect large numbers of other computers. During the day or two it takes for the antivirus vendors to release an update that addresses the newest viruses, every system is exposed.

Trojan Horse

A Trojan horse is named after the original Trojan horse of Greek mythology. It operates by appearing to be one thing, such as a game or a utility, but is in reality the tool of the Trojan horse's creator. In the Internet age, spoofed games are now replaced with programs such as SpyBlast,[6] which claim to protect against spyware when they *are* spyware themselves. Trojan horses can do a number of destructive deeds or they can monitor your computer use so that it can report your activities to a hacker or advertiser. Some spyware programs actually install other spyware programs as their first order of business. Apparently, spyware makers pay each other for the installation of one another's software.

Worm

A worm is a self-replicating malicious program. It differs from a Trojan horse in that it does not pretend to be something else, and it differs from a virus in that it does not attach itself to programs and documents. A worm "lives" in a computer's memory and copies itself to and from floppy disks or over network connections. Worms not only cause damage via their direct action but can also consume a computer or network's resources to the point where other tasks are slowed or stopped.

What Viruses Do

A virus program must be triggered in some way so that its computer code can be carried out. Computer files that can execute code are called *executables* or *programs*. As a rule, data files are not capable of infecting your computer because they cannot execute code on your computer. That means that opening a text file (.txt), a sound file (.mp3), or simply viewing a graphics file (.jpg, .gif) will not cause your computer to become infected with the virus. For many years the rule of thumb was to be wary of files that were executable while treating data and text files as safe. The other guideline that users once relied on was to open only files when they knew the sender. Naturally, virus writers, knowing many users followed these rules of thumb, adapted their techniques so that their viruses appeared safe and/or from a trusted source.

It can be very difficult to know when something that appears to be a text file is actually an executable file because virus writers hide the file extension. For example, the file "safe.txt" may actually be "safe.txt.ssh." The ssh extension is one of Microsoft Window's file executable extensions that are by design hidden from the user. The days of being able to know the nature of a file attachment based on the file extension is over. That's one important reason you need an up-to-date antivirus program.

The reason why a virus writer don't create executable files with safe file extensions, such as "txt," is because when the user clicks on it to open it the operating system will open it up in the user's text editor because it also thinks the file is a text file. The result would be a screen full of computer code gibberish in your text editor—ugly, but not dangerous. It's also important to note that what were thought of as text files in the past, such as doc files, now have the ability to include dangerous macros. A *macro* is a script that automatically runs features of the program in

---

6. Doxdesk website: http://www.doxdesk.com/parasite/SpyBlast.html

which it operates. Surprisingly, macros can do far more than just type in boilerplate text; they can email documents or delete files.

Types of Viruses

Although there are tens of thousands of viruses, most have common traits that let them be placed into one of the following groups:

- Boot sector viruses
- File-infecting viruses
- Macro viruses

Boot Sector Viruses

Boot sector viruses only reside in specific parts of a computer known as the *boot sector*. The boot sector of a hard drive is the area where operating system-related programs are stored, to be read and executed by the computer when it is turned on. The virus sits in the boot sector of your computer's hard drive and gets loaded into memory before an antivirus program can be loaded. Cleaning such viruses from a computer usually requires that the system be booted from an emergency boot disk so that the virus does not have a chance to load. All antivirus vendors make the creation of an emergency boot disk part of their installation process.

File-Infecting Viruses

File-infecting viruses, or parasitic viruses, attach themselves to legitimate program and system files. Such "host" files usually have one of the following extensions: .com, .exe, .drv, .bin, .ovl, .sys. Once the host file is infected, the virus operates whenever the host program operates. Sometimes an antivirus program can safely remove the virus from the host files and at other times the only solution is the replacement of the file with an uninfected copy.

Macro Viruses

Macro viruses account for the majority of viruses today, and are the largest and fastest-growing virus type. They are transmitted primarily through email attachments, but can be transmitted through floppy disks, file transfers, and Web downloads.

The reason macro viruses are so widespread is that they use the built-in capabilities of an existing software application on the user's computer. Therefore, a Microsoft Word macro virus will use the Word program to infect other Word documents and to use Outlook's email features to send viruses to everyone in the infected person's Outlook address book. Without Word, a Word macro virus would be unable to operate. Why does Microsoft allow this to happen, you wonder? Macros and other forms of hidden code within Microsoft documents make it possible for Microsoft to offer advanced features. These behind-the-scenes activities allow for routine processes to be automated and for applications to communicate with each other. Many of the ease-of-use features we enjoy are the same features being used by virus writers to ease their tasks.

Methods of Infection

Most viruses today are transmitted through email. The macro virus frequently takes advantage of the user's email address book to send out infected messages to the victim's contacts. The newer viruses now use the address book to create a false "from" line. Sometimes the message's from line will be a name from the user's address book. At other times it may be a composite of two other addresses. For example, if you have john@abc.edu and sally@xyz.edu, the virus may create a from line of sally@abc.edu. This technique helps the virus to spread because the receiver of the infected message may think the "from" address looks familiar. Providing a false from line has the additional benefit of making it very difficult for the receiver to know who has been infected. While they can be fairly sure it must be someone they know, they cannot determine who.

Virus writers have not limited themselves to email and floppy disk transmission. Peer-to-peer systems that allow users to share information directly over the Internet, such as Kazaa, Gnutella, and Grokster, are rapidly growing threats. Given the popularity of peer-to-peer systems with students, you need to pay special attention to them. There are even viruses that affect cell phones. How critical the problem will be with cell phones has yet to be determined, but the potential for massive disruption is clearly possible. Another new trend is for viruses to come through the Internet browser when the user visits a specifically constructed website. These hacked websites are designed to take advantage of a specific weakness in the user's browser. The damage can be anything from reading files off the user's computer to actually taking control of the user's computer.

In the past, many virus writers wrote viruses to show their friends what they were capable of doing. Viruses were frequently part of some underground competition between hackers. Now organized crime is moving in. They have every incentive to remain quiet about their exploits because their objective is to compromise as many computers as possible and to keep the fact of their success quiet so the victims of their attacks don't clean up their computers. Computer experts believe that it's entirely possible for viruses to include computer code that would destroy data and perhaps make the computer nonfunctional.[7] Fortunately, victims are worth more alive than dead.

Organized crime is interested in taking over other people's computers for a variety of reasons. Identity theft and spamming are two of their principal objectives. By taking over the control of a computer, they can watch the user type in personal information and passwords to online banks, and so forth. They can also use hijacked computers to launch attacks against other computers or used them as part of a spam delivery network. These hijacked computers are called "zombie computers." While the number of zombie computers out there is not exactly known,

---

7. Awaiting the PC Killers, *ComputerWorld*, by R. L. Mitchell, August 22, 2005. Available at http://www.computerworld.com/securitytopics/security/story/0,10801,104083,00.html

other than that it is in the millions, we do know that much of email spam is sent via such computers. The last thing you want to have to do is to explain to the local authorities that it was your computer and not you that sent porno spam to the local school board members.

Avoiding Viruses

The best way to avoid getting a computer virus is to use common sense. It is always better to be safe than sorry when it comes to strange email messages or unknown floppy disks. Virus writers don't have to get everyone to fall for their tricks—even infecting a small percentage of users is enough to keep the virus spreading. The good news is that most viruses can be detected by a careful user.

In order to protect your computer and all the valuable data stored in it, you need to install antivirus software and keep it up to date. Other than common sense, no other form of protection is more important.

If your antivirus program does not come with anti-spyware functions, you need to obtain a separate anti-spyware program. Microsoft offers a program called Windows Defender for users of Windows 2000 and newer versions.

Up to a 1,000 new viruses are created and released over the Internet every month.[8] As a result, an antivirus program needs to have its "definition file" updated regularly so that it can spot all the new viruses. Most antivirus systems are helpless against viruses that come out after the last update of the definition file. Because viruses tend to spread within hours and days of their release, the antivirus vendors usually release a new definition file every day. Likewise, the user should consider updating the definition file daily.

Some email programs are configured by default to automatically execute scripts. While the capability of automatically running scripts was written as a product enhancement, the unintended consequence has been to give virus writers a new way to explore a victim's computer. One such example is the "I Love You" virus. Users would open their messages and unwittingly execute the hidden script. Few users realized that these scripts ran even when the preview pane was used to view the message. This is very different from the early years of the Internet when a user could only become infected by manually detaching and opening a file.

Antivirus Scanning Techniques

There are several scanning strategies you need to be aware of when using antivirus software. *On-demand scanning* is the scanning of a file (or email) whenever it is opened or closed. It is a useful "everyday" virus protection strategy. *Full scanning* involves the scanning of all files and programs on your hard drive. This process is far more resource-consuming because the antivirus software scans everything on your machine, and requires a significant amount of system memory and

---

8. Looking into the mind of a virus writer, CNN.com/Technology, March 19, 2003, Reuters. Available at http://edition.cnn.com/2003/TECH/internet/03/19/virus.writers.reut/index.html

processing power. As a result, full scanning is usually done occasionally, such as once a week. Of course, if the background scanning is keeping your system clean, the full scan should be a formality—but a formality worth taking.

Because antivirus software works in the background, users may become so accustomed to not seeing the antivirus program that they don't notice when the antivirus program is not running. Don't assume the program is running or that the virus definitions are current. Check it every now and then. Look to make sure your license is still current. Some antivirus programs will simply stop updating after you license has expired. Licenses are usually issued a year at a time. And some viruses turn off the antivirus software so as to work unhindered.

Virus Definitions

Antivirus programs require updates to their "definitions" to ensure that the software is capable of discovering new versions of viruses when they arrive at your machine. Virus definitions are descriptions that the antivirus software uses to search for viruses on your machine. Many antivirus software companies have a database of known viruses that are usually updated daily or weekly. Given the rapidity with which the newest viruses spread, daily updating is a wise precaution. In fact, you should manually force an update right after starting up the computer if there are alerts about a particularly worrisome new virus. If your version of antivirus software does not include support for spyware detection, you should either upgrade or obtain a third-party antispyware program.

There are several methods of updating the virus definitions. Depending on the software you are using, you can choose from the following:

- **Auto-update:** Enabling this feature will enable the antivirus software to automatically visit the antivirus vendor's website, check for any new virus threats, and then update your software with new virus definitions.
- **Remind:** By enabling this feature and setting up a designated reminder time, the antivirus software will ensure that you don't forget to check for new virus definitions.
- **Manual:** This feature should be used for forced updates between regularly scheduled updates rather than the only method for updating definitions. For example, you just heard of a new virus spreading quickly over the Internet. If your next update is not for another day or two, force an update using the manual method.

11

Lurking Dangers

Some of the most serious security concerns are the ones that you may not even know about. Obviously, no one is going to check on the security of a process if it's not known as a source of risk. This chapter looks at the dangers of file sharing, telephones, the disposal of old computers and trash, wireless networks, and physical security.

File Sharing: Sharing More Than You Know

Kazaa and similar file-sharing programs work on the basis that each user is both a server and client. Young people may understand that they are "sharing" someone else's Madonna song, but they may not understand that they too are sharing. These systems typically work by creating a file-sharing area on the user's hard disk. Files the user downloads plus anything else that is in this shared area are open to all other users of the network. Because many users don't understand the Faustian pact they have made, they leave documents they would never want to be shared in the shared area of their disk. If this is not bad enough, many of these file-sharing networks also operate as spyware.

A leading security magazine did an experiment with Kazaa in October 2003 to see how many sensitive documents Kazaa users were intentionally exposing. In less than 2 hours they found:

- Restricted access to Boeing 737 and 777 flight manuals (more than 5,000 pages) for a major U.S. Airline;
- A plethora of end-user password lists in Word documents, including passwords for bank, student loan, frequent flyer, and various email accounts;
- Case histories of various psychiatric patients;
- Divorce strategy and litigation for a couple whose relationship was on the rocks.[9]

---

9. 2003: The Security Year in Review, *Secure Computing Magazine*, by B. Rothke, December, 2003. Available at http://www.scmagazine.com/scmagazine/2003_12/feature_1/

Telephones

While the computer gets most of the attention in the press regarding security, the modern office is replete with security concerns. Phone fraud is both common and expensive. Any school with a telephone system needs to ask the telephone vendor to explain the system's security provisions. This is a conversation that rarely happens without a specific request. In many ways, the office telephone system is more vulnerable than the computer network. It is all too easy to assume that your school's phone system is just a bigger version of your home phone. In fact, a better comparison would be one with your telephone company. The term *PBX*, the controlling unit for your telephone system, means *Private Branch Exchange*.

Attackers seek to obtain remote control over PBXs so that they can sell "cheap calls" to their "customers." While the criminal's customers get cheap calls to their long-distance locations, your school's next telephone bill will be anything but cheap. Organizations have lost hundreds of thousands of dollars over just a few weeks. And, unlike a stolen calling card with its liability cap of $50, PBX-based phone fraud comes with unlimited liability.

Disposing of Old Computers

Eventually every computer will leave your ownership. Whether you put it in the trash or donate it to someone even poorer than you, the data on the hard drive is almost certainly retrievable. Deleting files or formatting the disk is no guarantee that the data is gone.

If you are going to send the unit to the trash, you should consider removing the hard disk and smashing it with a large hammer. Even "dead" hard drives can have data extracted if the right equipment is used. In the unfortunate case that a hard drive has died and no backup has been made—a situation that should not happen—there are data-recovery firms that can usually retrieve the data. Their data recovery prices are high, but the key point to remember is that your data is recoverable.

If the unit is going to be donated, erase the hard drive using a secure wipe-disk utility. These utilities make sure that all the data is overwritten and deleted to U.S. government specifications. Of course, if the unit was not used for sensitive information, formatting the drive and reinstalling the operating system is adequate.

If you do decide to donate a computer, you need to be clear about which programs can be legally installed. For instance, if you used your old software to build a new computer, sending out the old computer with that software installed could make your new computer illegal. It's generally safe to install the operating system and leave it at that.

Trash

One of the most common ways hackers and criminals get computer information is by rummaging through an organization's trash bin. This practice, colorfully known as "dumpster diving," takes advantage of the fact that people often print drafts of sensitive documents and then toss them away.

Sensitive paper-based information should always be shredded. Shredders come in many sizes and are a variety of prices. In some locations, one large shredder makes sense while in other environments, having a number of smaller shredders may be more desirable. Larger shredders have the advantage of being faster. They pull the paper through faster and can take more pieces of paper at the same time. Smaller shredders can be a good choice if users are unlikely to use the larger shredder consistently due to the inconvenience of having to walk too far. Another solution is to have a trash basket next to each person's desk exclusively for paper. At the end of the day the baskets are emptied for shredding. Whatever works is the best solution for your organization.

If your information is very sensitive, be aware that not all shredders destroy documents with equal results. The lower-priced units tend to cut the paper into strips that can be put back together—especially the greenbar paper used for financial reports. More expensive shredders cut the paper in two directions—cross-cut—resulting in a pile of tiny paper squares.

Wireless Networks

Wireless networking is a hot technology. Wireless networks are very useful when traditional wiring is not practical or a temporary network needs to be created. The downside is that they are frequently not secure. Some would argue that it has been only recently that a high level of security was even possible. The good news is that the newer wireless devices are secure when configured correctly.

One of the major security problems with wireless networks is that their reach doesn't stop at your property line. It's entirely possible that people in the next building or sitting in a car parked on the street are accessing your network. Unlike attackers over the Internet, these users would be on your local area network—behind your firewall. Even if your uninvited users have no evil intent, they are using your computer network and your Internet connection. If your users have "file and printer sharing" turned on, it is possible for an uninvited visitor to access the shared files.

In situations where a wire can work, use it. But there are many situations, such as on the campus's grounds, where only wireless will do. Wireless networks have a well-deserved reputation for not being secure. Primarily, this has been due to the fact that most systems come with all the security features turned off to make them easier to install. The first action you should take after installation is to turn on the security features. There are many security futures possible, but the WPA feature is the first wireless security feature considered truly secure. But any security feature is better than none. There are so many open wireless networks that even the smallest hindrance will often be enough to discourage freeloaders from joining your network.

Physical Security

The most elaborate protection system isn't much good if all your data is stolen in a robbery. Physical security not only involves protection against robbery and fire, but also against physical access to the computers by unauthorized individuals.

Critical systems should ideally be behind locked doors. This limits unauthorized access and reduces the dangers of casual theft. In some cases, critical data, such as accounting and personnel information, should be stored on an external hard disk that can be stored in a safe or taken home at the end of the day.

As difficult as it is to protect a computer attached to the Internet, it is far more difficult to protect a computer when the attacker has physical access to the system. This is especially a concern for laptop computers as they frequently contain sensitive information and are popular targets for thieves. Thieves are quite aware that laptops often contain sensitive information that can be sold to other parties.

A determined thief is very difficult to stop. Computers should be anchored to desks and other heavy objects via cables, special plates, and super-strong glues. You may need to consider devices that lock the computer case so that thieves cannot steal internal components. When physical security is strong, thieves will target a less vigilant neighbor.

12

Hoaxes and Spam

Hoaxes and spam are usually seen as little more than annoyances. In reality, they are serious security concerns. While the obvious purpose of spam is to get you to buy something, spam has a variety of secondary effects that are security concerns.

Spammers aren't just interested in selling you their products; they want to know if your email address is valid. Anything they can do to identify active email addresses is of monetary value to them either for their own spamming efforts or for selling to other spammers. One of the easiest ways to let a spammer know that your email address is working is for you to send them a request to be removed from their list. They love that. *Never do this*. Not only will this fail to get you off their list, but soon you'll be receiving even more spam as the spammer sells your now-validated address to other spammers.

The simple act of opening a spam message may validate your address. Spam messages frequently contain code that will automatically contact the spammer's server when the message has been opened. Naturally, this connection by your email program informs the spammer that your address is valid. In fact, not only does the spammer know that your address is valid, but they know that you are the type of person who opens spam messages. Furthermore, your connection to their system provides them with the IP address of your computer. Pretty soon you'll be getting spam regionalized to your location. Most Internet users assume that their location is anonymous. If you believe this, visit a service such as IP2LOCATION (http://www.ip2location.com/). This site can tell you what part of the world you're connecting to the Internet from.

The dramatic increase in the amount of spam is now becoming a security concern simply because it clogs email accounts to the point where legitimate messages bounce and Internet connections slow to the point of being unusable. Until everyone who receives spam messages decides never to purchase what is offered, spammers will continue to function. Since spammers send out hundreds of millions of messages a day, even a fraction of 1% response is profitable—especially given that they don't pay for sending their messages.

In August 2005 AOL sued one young boy in New Hampshire who had sent tens of millions of messages to AOL users. As a result of AOL's lawsuit the kid had to turn over his Hummer and large amounts of cash and gold bars. He had 40 employees filling orders for him.[10] Think of this kid next time you say no one

---

10. Spammer's Loot, America Online Press Center, 2005. Available at http://corp.aol.com/press/media_spammersloot.shtml

would be stupid enough to buy what spammers are selling. Below are some tips for reducing the amount of spam you receive.

1. Use more than one email address—one for business, one for friends, and another one for public use. The public one can used for a situation where you know your email address will be "harvested" by spammers, such as chat rooms, public discussion boards, and domain name registration forms.
2. Listing your email address on a website is asking to be spammed. You can protect yourself by disguising your email address. For example "jbrown@abc.org" could be "jbrown at abc.org." The spammer's automated robot programs probably won't understand it, but human visitors will. Another simple technique is to create your email address as an image and put it on the web page. The user won't see any difference, but an automated scanner will not be able to read the graphic image.
3. Use one of many anti-spam programs to scan your incoming email messages. You can expect them to identify approximately 90% of spam messages. Rates higher than 90% are possible, but as you get closer to 100% success the chance of mislabeling legitimate messages increases. If you want the highest level of protection, you can use one of the programs that only lets in email from approved senders. An email coming from an unknown address has an email message sent back to the sender asking him or her to verify his or her identity. This is normally done by having the sender type in a code displayed in a graphic image. Automated systems cannot read these images and spammers are not going to spend time reading these challenges. This system, while effective, may be too limiting for business use.
4. Some ISPs (Internet Service Providers) offer anti-spam services. If yours does, there is no good reason not to use it.
5. If you run your own email server, there are anti-spam programs that can be added. Some of the best anti-spam systems for servers are free of charge. (For example: SpamAssassin http://spamassassin.org.)
6. There are now third-party email services that will clean email of viruses and spam before relaying it onto your email server. These systems can be very effective but the cost for a school might be prohibitive. Of course, it may not be an issue if your system is being made unusable from the heavy volume of spam and virus-infected messages. One of the advantages of an external solution is that your Internet line is not burdened with spam messages. This is a significant benefit if your Internet line is expensive.

Some spam is so upsetting that you want to complain about it. Unfortunately, it is usually not worth the effort. The main problem is that email messages are very easy to fake. Without expert knowledge of how to read an email header, it is very likely that you'll complain to the wrong people. (The header is where all the to, from, times, etc., are kept). If you want to know how to read an email header, there are a number of sites on the Internet that provide instructions on how to read an email header. Your best option is to send the spam message along with its header to the United States Federal Trade Commission spam center: uce@ftc.gov.

Phishing

Phishing comes from the word *fishing*. Too bad you're the fish. With phishing, hackers create a website that appears to represent some provider you deal with, perhaps an online banking site, eBay, or Paypal. They then attempt to lure you to their fake site using spam messages—of course, you don't know it's part of a mass mailing. Phishing email messages attempt to look like real messages from trusted sources. While most of the recipients don't have an eBay or a Citibank account, those who do may be duped into thinking the message is legitimate.

A Phisher's object is to get you to visit a website that you believe belongs to your bank or some other business with which you have an account. Once you have attempted to log in to their fake site, the hacker has your username and password for the real site. They quickly go into your account as you and steal your money or your identity.

It is often difficult to know when a site is a phishing site because the hackers steal the graphics and text of the real site. Generally, no reputable firm will ask you to do anything important via email. Such a request should immediately make you suspicious. Call the supposed source of the email for confirmation. Check the URL in the message to make sure it is exactly the one for your firm. For example, a phishing site pretending to be Citibank might use www.citybank.com when it should be www.citibank.com. Or perhaps www.aol.com is represented by www.ao1.com. The letter "l" being substituted with an 1 (one).

Below is the URL for a site that monitors known phishing sites. Phishing sites tend not to be up for very long because the firms being phished are naturally very energitic about closing down the phishing sites. So your best defense is to be suspicious. Visit http://www.fraudwatchinternational.com/internetfraud/phishing.htm for more information.

If you believe you have been the victim of a phishing site, you need to contact the real firm immediately and have your password changed.

Hoaxes

Just as some individuals get some form of perverse pleasure out of writing viruses, others apparently enjoy distributing false information. Hoaxes differ from phishing email messages in that the main goal is to fool the reader rather than to steal anything. Hoaxes are not always harmless, however. In one hoax, for example, the reader is informed that their computer has been infected by a terrible virus that "no antivirus system can stop." As proof of its claim, it tells the user to look for a specific file name on their computer. Any reader on a Windows-based computer will find this file because it is a legitimate part of Windows. The now-panicked user deletes this file and then emails the hoax's warning to everyone they know so that they can be "helped," too. The result can be hours of staff time fixing the damage users have inflicted on their computers.

Not all hoaxes are about viruses. Some may spread false information. One hoax reported that a sick child would certainly recover from some dire disease if they could only receive a million email messages.

And, of course, the original hoax, the good ole chain letter, has made a smooth transition to the Internet. Just remember that if one person sends a chain email to

10 people and each recipient does the same, there will be a million email messages sent out in the sixth round. Email may be free to the user, but the server capacity and Internet bandwidth that supports their free email is not "free" for you.

Here is what hoax-busting websites have to say regarding the essential characteristics of a hoax:

- **Hyperbole about damage that will be inflicted:** For example:

  "will wreak terrible havoc on your computer"
  "this is a very dangerous virus, much worse than Melissa and there is NO remedy for it at this time"
  "unparalleled in its destructive capability"
  "I received this virus and it wiped me out."
  "Other, more well-known viruses such as . . . pale in comparison to the prospects of this newest creation by a warped mentality."

  Sometimes these warnings specifically mention that the alleged virus will destroy hardware (e.g., hard disk drives). While it is possible to write malicious programs to damage some types of hardware, physical damage to hardware is rare. Most commonly, malicious programs only delete files or alter data in files, without harming the disk drive itself.

- **Frantic style.** For example:

  Many exclamation marks in the text of the message or in the subject line.
  Use of all UPPER-CASE letters.
  Excessive use of boldface or italics.
  Use of larger-than-normal-sized letters in the message.

  The use of hyperbole or a frantic style is symptomatic of a hoax, because scientists, engineers, and professional technical writers use neither hyperbole nor frantic style.

- **Technical details that appear to give the message credibility.** Someone who is knowledgeable about computer science or electrical engineering can often spot errors or implausible statements in the message, but most readers do not have the technical background to evaluate such content. The point made here is that inclusion of technical terms is not proof that the author is either correct or sincere.

  Sometimes the message contains long, detailed instructions for removing the alleged virus. Such instructions are needless, as it would be easier to refer the reader to the URL of the appropriate webpage at a major antivirus vendor's website. Putting long, detailed instructions into an email is a symptom of a hoax.

- **Appeal to authority.** Hoaxes often mention the name of a major corporation (e.g., IBM or Microsoft) or a government agency (e.g., FCC) that has allegedly originally issued or endorsed the message. Alternatively, the hoax might mention the name of a major antivirus software vendor. A key feature of a hoax is the lack of a URL that would allow the reader to confirm the source of the information.

- Last, and perhaps most importantly, **the hoax will urge you to forward this message** immediately to everyone you know. If you believe the hoax is credible, this encouragement plays on your desire to be helpful to other people, particularly your friends, colleagues, clients. . . . In fact, if you forward a hoax, you are contributing to panic, and possibly encouraging someone else to harm his or her computer.

    Before you forward the message:

    Check one or more of the antivirus vendors' websites listed below to see if the message is a known hoax.

    If you work in a major corporation, forward the message to the computer center or information technology department and let them decide whether to warn other users. If you can not evaluate the technical content of a message warning about a new computer virus, then it is not your job to warn others about this alleged new virus.[11]

The websites listed below have databases of known hoaxes. Another method is simply to put in the suspected hoaxes subject line into an Internet search engine, such as Google.com, and see if the results of the search identify the message as fraudulent.

http://hoaxbusters.ciac.org/
http://vil.mcafee.com/hoax.asp
http://www.symantec.com/avcenter/hoax.html
http://www.vmyths.com/

---

11. Computer Virus Hoaxes, by R. B. Standler, June 15, 2002. Available at http://www.rbs2.com/choax.htm

13

Firewalls

The term *firewall* is used in several areas of our normal, everyday lives. In a car, a firewall is a barrier placed between the main passenger cabin and the engine compartment. In case of a fire, the firewall protects the passengers in the car by not permitting fire to enter the passenger cabin.

A computer firewall functions similarly to a car firewall. It prevents fires from spreading, but in this case, the fire is a malicious attacker trying to do one of the following:

- Vandalize your network or website,
- Crash your network or computer,
- Steal or alter data, and,
- Use your computer to attack other computers or to send spam.

The key to all these activities is access to your computers. A firewall's basic function is to keep unauthorized users on the outside of your network from getting in. The attacker's goal is to become a user on your system. Because the simplest solution of cutting all connections to the outside world is not feasible, the firewall attempts to distinguish between legitimate communications coming in from the outside world and those illegitimate forms of communications.

The firewall acts as a sieve, filtering communication traffic entering and leaving your network. If an attempt at communication is flagged as unacceptable, it is blocked.

Firewalls use something called an *access control policy* to determine what is and isn't allowed. An access control policy is a list of rules describing the who, what, and when of all communication passing through the firewall. The first rules on the typical firewall are to "let everything out and block everything from the outside." From here, the person responsible for the firewall creates rules that make specific exceptions. For example, if you have an email server, you will need a rule that says that email traffic can come through the firewall as long as it is going to the email server. Likewise, if you want to block the students from using instant messaging, you will need to add an exception to the rule that allows all outbound traffic.

Shortcomings of Firewalls

As important as firewalls are, they are not perfect. Too many people assume that because they have a firewall, nothing bad can happen to them. Here are some considerations to keep in mind:

- Most firewalls will not check for viruses, spyware, or other dangerous applications. Frequently, these services can now be added with an additional purchase from the firewall vendor.
- Most firewalls do not protect web and email servers from attacks on the applications that run the web and email services. In other words, your public web server must be open to the public by definition. The software that runs the website thus could be vulnerable to attack.
- Firewalls, like any computer, can have bugs or weaknesses that allow an attacker to take control of it.
- Firewalls can provide a false sense of security.
- Firewalls do little to protect the network from security breaches that originate from inside the network.

Firewall Types

There are a variety of firewall solutions to choose from, and each of these different firewall solutions has its positives and negatives. In this section, we will discuss the different firewall solutions available to the users both at the school and at home. Don't overlook protecting your staff's home computers, given that this is a frequent route for viruses and other security issues to enter the school.

There are two primary types of firewalls: hardware-based and software-based.

Software-Based Firewalls

Software-based firewalls, also called *personal firewalls*, run directly on the user's computer. It used to be the case that these firewalls were an inexpensive solution for the home user who did not want to purchase a hardware firewall. Today, however, firewalls that run on the user's computer offer forms of protection that an external hardware-based firewall is unable to provide.

Personal firewalls have the advantage of knowing which application on the user's computer is attempting to communicate. This is because the firewall can monitor the operating system and thus determine which program is attempting communication. As the program starts to communicate, the personal firewall will ask the user to permit or block the program. This monitoring of local programs is critical for stopping spyware and Trojan horses.

The major downside to personal firewalls is that most users don't know the difference between legitimate programs and spyware. The firewall doesn't ask "Do you want to allow Windows to communicate with the Internet?"; rather, it will ask something like, "Do you want to allow svchost.exe to contact the Internet?" The good news is that personal firewall programs are now coming with extensive lists of good and bad programs so that the user does not need to be an expert.

Hardware-Based Firewalls

Hardware-based firewalls usually run a separate piece of hardware that protects groups of computers, such as a school's network. When people talk about firewalls, it is usually these external devices to which they are referring. For simplicity's sake, I'll refer to all hardware-based firewalls as just *firewalls*.

Every school should have a dedicated firewall. While personal firewalls are great, they don't protect what they don't run on. For example, your networked printer doesn't come with a firewall. If a computer was for some reason to lose its personal firewall, it would be in great danger if no other firewall was in place. Given the price of firewalls, there is no reason that even home users should be without a dedicated firewall.

Just as personal firewalls can provide valuable functions that only they can do, hardware-based firewalls can likewise provide services that personal firewalls cannot. The most of valuable of these services is Network Address Translation.

Network Address Translation (NAT)

Most firewalls provide a service called "Network Address Translation" (NAT). NAT allows the firewall to share a single Internet address with an entire network. When Internet service is established with the Internet Service Provider (ISP), the ISP provides one or more Internet addresses. Because there is a shortage of Internet addresses, the ISP tends to give users as few addresses as possible. Firewalls alleviate this restriction by providing their own set of Internet addresses for the computers on the network behind them. These addresses are known as *private addresses*. These firewall-supplied addresses are private in that they only exist on the local network, whereas addresses that can be used on the Internet are public addresses. The firewall has a public address and knows the identity of all the devices with private addresses. The primary purpose of NAT is to translate the identity between the private and public addresses. This translation between the "private" numbers inside the network and the external address allows the office to have unlimited numbers of computers inside the network without having to purchase more public addresses from the ISP.

Below are the possible private addresses ranges used by NAT (ordered by potential size of local network: large/medium/small).

10.0.0.0—10.255.255.255
172.16.0.0—172.31.255.255
192.168.0.0—192.168.255.255

The use of private numbers provides a significant level of protection against Internet attacks because hackers have a much more difficult time attacking a computer that uses a private address. Private addresses cannot traverse the public Internet. This restriction allows unlimited numbers of local networks to use the same private addresses without fear of conflict with one another. You can think of it like an internal phone system in a hotel. There are thousands of phones in hotels with "705" as a number. But, because the number "705" doesn't mean anything on the public telephone network, there is no conflict between the hotels. So when a hacker attempts to directly address your computer's private address, the Internet cannot deliver it.

DHCP

DHCP (Dynamic Host Configuration Protocol) has already been covered, but it's a feature that is frequently operated by the firewall. DHCP works with NAT by allocating private addresses. Whereas NAT has to run on the firewall, DHCP can run on separate devices. For anything other than very large schools, there is probably no reason not to use the firewall for this service.

Firewall Testing

A firewall that isn't working well is akin to forgetting to lock the front door to your house as you go to work. You think you're safe until you find out otherwise. There are ways to test your firewall to make sure it is doing what you expect it to do. The easiest way is to use a free service offered by Gibson Research. Go to the following URL while on a computer behind the firewall you want tested. Press the "Probe My Ports!" button. Their system will run a test against your firewall and will let you know if any "doors" are left unlocked. (https://grc.com/x/ne.dll?bh0bkyd2)

14

Backup Strategies

The process of data protection is analogous to being in the army: long periods of tedium followed by brief periods of emergency. There are few ways more effective for getting dismissed from a technical job than to botch the protection of your school's data.

What Is a Backup?

A backup is any process that creates a second copy of data. The purpose of a backup is to ensure that when something goes wrong on your machine—and chances are high that at some time something will go wrong—the time and money that went into creating the documents on your system are not lost. Essentially, a backup is made to prevent hardware, software, and human failures from harming valuable computer data. A good backup strategy combined with a workable disaster plan should be able to handle even the worst-case scenarios.

Inside your computer there are many different things going on at any given time. As with anything complex, something will eventually go wrong. Whether a hardware component fails, you accidentally delete or overwrite a file, a power surge hits, or your computer is stolen, knowing that all the lost data can be restored gives you peace of mind—and job security.

Here are a few important terms associated with data protection:

- **Archiving:** This is the process of copying a file or files onto a storage medium (such as a backup tape) for long-term storage. Generally, the original version is removed so as to make space for current work.
- **Restoration:** This is the process of copying stored data to a place where it can be worked on. Generally, this means the data is copied back to its original location, but this is not a requirement.

What Should You Back Up?

Your operating system and software applications usually come on an installation CD-ROM. It's not a bad idea to make copies of the installation CD-ROMs and store the masters somewhere else. If they are lost or damaged, many vendors will not replace them for you.

While a complete backup will allow you to restore the operating system and software applications, there are situations where the installation disks will be required to install new features or to repair damaged files. Attempting to restore a single program from a tape backup is probably a fruitless endeavor due to the complexity involved with most installations. This is especially true with Windows applications.

The data on your machine (all the files you create using the software, such as accounting files or letters) should be backed up regularly. These files are where all your hard work and time are represented. Without them you could be lost, or at the very least you would have to spend countless hours trying to replace or recreate them.

Strategies for Backing Up

You will need to decide how often and what to back up. There are several strategies for backing up files:

- **Full backup:** This involves making a backup copy of everything. This method is the easiest in terms of configuration, because there is not selection between what to back up and what not to bother with. However, this method is the most time-consuming because a backup system has to copy every file.
- **Incremental backup:** This involves making a backup copy of only the files that have been altered since the last backup. This method is faster than a full backup. New data is defined as either new files or old files that have changed.
- **Differential backup:** This method is a combination of both the full backup and incremental backup strategies. This method requires two backup devices: one for full backups, and the other for incremental backups. With this strategy, you will always have a recent full backup on one storage medium and any recent changes on the other storage medium.

Remember that regardless of the strategy you choose to employ, making regular backups is vital to ensuring that your data is always safe—and that is the primary purpose of a backup. The strategy you choose to back up your data is less important than actually making regular backups. It's only when one gets into truly massive file storage situations that the difference between backup methodologies comes into play.

Backup Devices

There are many different devices that can be used to back up the data on your machine. Each device has its own set of benefits and drawbacks, so it is important to determine how important your data is, how much data you have, and how much money you are willing to spend to ensure that your data is safe. The following is a list of some of the backup devices and memory storage mediums available for data backup.

Iomega Rev

This is a 36-gig removable drive that compares favorably with tape systems and is not too much more expensive than Iomega's 750 meg Zip drive product.

CD-RW

The rewritable CD is one of the more recent backup technologies. While the cost of a rewritable CD is relatively low, the speed of writing is slow, and the size of storage isn't nearly as large as some of the other products, such as a digital tape. However, compared to a Zip drive, the CD-RW's 650 MB (or larger) storage capacity is more than adequate for most systems, and its ability to play multimedia files is also a plus. In addition, the CD-RW drive can be used in place of a traditional CD-ROM drive, making it even more useful.

DVD drives have already started to replace CD-ROMs. With the recent release of a new high-capacity 50-gig DVD system, it will not be long before using CD-ROMs for backups will disappear. CD-ROMs are still preferred for sending data through the mail and for small backups.

Floppy Disk

A floppy disk stores a mere 1.44 MB of data but has the virtue of being easy to use, readily available, and inexpensive. It is a good option for backing up a few document files, and a particularly good idea when you are working on a few important documents and you are not sure the person responsible for backups is doing a good job.

The limitations of the floppy disk are obvious, but why spend hundreds of dollars on a high-end device if you only need to back up a few Word documents? Another plus is that most computers come with a floppy disk drive already installed. This is not true of most every other backup system. However, the severe size limitations make floppy disks useless for storing large numbers of files, or even a single large file such as a desktop publishing file. Just remember to be careful how you handle floppy disks given that heat, spilled coffee, and small magnets can destroy the disk or erase the data on the disk.

There are some situations were the USB keys can replace floppy disks. In many cases, this is a great choice, but when it comes to situations where you have to give away the storage medium along with the data, you'll want to give away a floppy before you give away your USB device. The only other viable way to give away information is to burn a CD-ROM.

Low-End Tape Solutions

The main advantage of using tape is its good cost/capacity ratio. The main disadvantage is that many companies make tape units, and compatibility between them is not assured. Tapes suffer from the sequential nature of how data is stored. This means that the tape drive cannot access a specific file or directory without first reading, or least rolling past, all the data that precedes it on the tape. You can think of it as being like the difference between a movie on DVD and the same movie on a VHS tape. If you want to get to a specific scene in the movie, the DVD allows you to go directly there because the entire movie is equally accessible to the DVD player. The VHS player, however, has to fast-forward the tape to the correct location before it can access the required scene.

Supplemental Hard Disks

Prices for hard disks have gone down so much that backing up to another drive may be the best solution. Naturally, a hard disk that's inside one of your computers does nothing for you if your office has a fire and all the equipment is destroyed. There are removable hard drives that can be taken out and stored in a safe location.

When to Back Up

The rule of thumb for when to backup is, If you would miss it if it were gone, back it up. This means that data that does not change frequently, like a reference database, may only need to be backed up once. Making repeated backups of the same data wastes storage space. On the other hand, data that is vital and changes quickly may require real-time or near-real-time backing up. No one wants to be the patient in the hospital who did not get his or her medicine because the hospital's file server crashed 5 minutes after the doctor's prescription was entered.

Real-Time Backups

Sometimes "soon" is not soon enough for backing up critical data. Continuous data protection is not nearly as difficult as it sounds. An easy method is to install a second hard disk of similar capacity to the first disk and mirror it. "Mirror" does what it sounds like: anything that happens on the first drive is done simultaneously on the second drive. Another term for *mirror* is RAID 1 (RAID stands for Redundant Array of Inexpensive/Independent Drives). The "1" refers to one of ten or so possible RAID configurations. Given the low cost of drives, there are very few reasons why you would not use mirroring for servers and other important locations of data.

A higher level of RAID in common use is that of RAID 5. RAID 5 frequently uses five to ten disk drives—as opposed to RAID 1's two drives. Each drive stores

Figure 16. RAID 5 Diagram

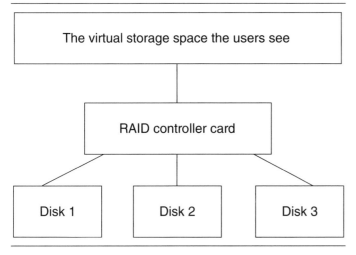

some information about the other drives. If any single drive dies, the other disks can duplicate the data. RAID 5 has some additional benefits over those of mirroring. First, a RAID 5 system can grow in data storage size far beyond that of a single drive. Mirror, by contrast, does not increase storage size at all. Second, RAID systems are faster than single drives because reading and writing from storage is shared between multiple disks.

Sometimes you want to have a second computer ready to take over the instant your primary system dies. In these situations you can use "hot" backups. These are servers that act as mirrors for another computer. When the primary computer dies, the second system takes over. Of course, the expense of having a second server doing nothing on its own can be significant. You will need to check with the software vendors you use to see if you have to pay for the copy on the second server. In many cases you will. So not only will you be paying double for your server, but you also have to add fairly expensive hardware and software for connecting the two servers. This connection not only transmits data from the first to the second computer, but determines when the first server has died and the second computer needs to take over. This all happens in real-time. If you require the highest levels of reliability, this is a method worth considering.

All real-time backups share a common problem: anything bad that happens to the original also happens to the copy. If the system is totally corrupted by a virus, the mirrored copy will faithfully reproduce the corruption. If you have a requirement for both real-time data protection and cannot wait for the nightly backup to make a noncorruptible version, the solution is *content versioning*. A CVS (Concurrent Version System) makes a backup of every change, but it keeps previous versions. This can be very important when something bad happened but you cannot be sure when. A CVS allows you to go back to each previous version until you find a safe version.

15

When Things Go Wrong

If you have reason to think your system has been compromised, you must take immediate action. It is better to waste some time checking whether you have been compromised than to assume you are safe and later find out that your data has been deleted or your system is under the control of some remote attacker.

Get Offline

Getting offline is the first course of action to take when you suspect your system has been compromised. Disconnect your computer from the network: unplug any phone lines and network cables; if you have a wireless network, remove the wireless network card or turn off your access point. If you have a broadband Internet connection, it is probably a good idea to disconnect it from the external Internet connection as well.

This act of isolating the suspect computer from the network achieves several goals:

- If an attacker is still trying to gain access to your computer, you will stop her or him in her or his tracks.
- If an attacker has gained access to your system, you deny him that access while the system is disconnected from the network.
- If a worm has infected your system (such as an email worm like Melissa), disconnecting your computer will stop it from spreading any further.
- If a Trojan horse is active on your system and sending information to its author, you stop it by disconnecting from the network.

Now that you have bought yourself some time you can proceed with care to diagnose the problem and resolve it.

Have I Been Compromised?

Look for symptoms of an attack when you suspect that your system may have been compromised. Some of these symptoms are obvious, while others are subtle, obscure, and easily missed. Some of the obvious signs that you have been compromised by an attacker include the following:

- Your system appears to be operating on its own, as if controlled by an unseen person. The unseen person may be the attacker. Be careful here, though, because many of today's programs carry out processes in the background. For example, antivirus programs are often set to download update files at specific times.
- Your system seems to run unbearably slowly at all times, even when you are not running any applications. An attacker could be using your computer to conduct resource-intensive computing tasks. Once again, this could also be the result of an application gone haywire. Restart the computer and see if the behavior continues. If it does, this is a more serious indication of a problem. It may be as simple as your computer running out of hard disk space. When a hard drive runs out of space, it has to do extra work. This slows the computer greatly and may produce an audible thrashing sound.
- Your passwords seem to magically change and you can't log into your computer. Check to make sure your caps-lock key is off—a frequent cause of misentered passwords.
- You discover new user accounts have been created that you know for a fact did not previously exist. Make sure no one has made them before suspecting an attacker.
- Files or directories magically disappear. The attacker could have deleted them. You should also consider running a scan of the hard disk to make sure there isn't a hard disk failure damaging the content. If you are using multiple computers, some computers may be set to show "hidden" directories while other computers may not.
- New mail messages that you have not previously read are marked as read; in this case, it seems as though an attacker could be monitoring your emails. This is unlikely, given that someone reading your mail could easily reset the "read" flag back to "unread." Yet it could be indicative that a less sophisticated person, such as a student, took advantage of you leaving your email program on the screen unattended.

Many attacks are not even this obvious. As with all things, prevention is preferable to the cure. If you have a strong suspicion that your system has been compromised in such a way that your attacker has full control of the system, you should completely rebuild the system. This means formatting the hard disk and installing from the installation disks. You may not know when the breach took place, so restoring to a previous point in time may not remove the attacker. Sophisticated hackers have the ability to remove evidence of their activities and to plant innocuous files that will allow them in at a later point.

Virus Infections

Even if you have taken every precaution, your system may still become infected by a virus, a Trojan horse, or a worm. You have to assume that the virus may have corrupted or turned off your antivirus program. You need to check your system using a "clean" virus checker.

To do this, you need to use a rescue disk or rescue disk set that you created when you installed your virus software. The rescue disk will be an option when you install any antivirus program. It would be a mistake to bypass this option.

Computers That Won't Boot

There are many other possible causes for a computer that won't boot. *Booting* can be defined as the process that starts with turning on the power and ends with the operating system finishing its loading. Some causes are extremely simple to resolve while others require you to purchase a new unit. Below are some of common reasons a computer will not boot.

- The disk might be corrupted due to a software bug or a hardware failure.
- The hard disk's cable might have come loose inside the computer case.
- The computer's power supply might be damaged or unplugged. Check to make sure that the power cord is firmly plugged in. An unplugged unit is perhaps the most common reason a computer does not start. Some power cords can become loose or stop making a good connection with the electrical prongs. Try another cord.
- The computer's basic input/output system (BIOS, the computer's built-in program that starts the computer and loads the operating system) might be corrupted and need to be re-flashed. This requires a special software utility provided by the manufacturer of your BIOS chip.
- The computer's memory might be bad. Pulling out the memory chips and reinserting them can sometimes fix the problem.

The first step is to determine exactly where the boot process is failing. Here are some critical points in the boot process. These steps are in sequential order.

1. **Power light:** When the On button is pressed, does any light come on or do you hear the fan? The unit may not be plugged in, or maybe a fuse was blown somewhere. One possibility to consider is that the On button is broken. Sometimes the computer case will pull away from computer's internal frame in such a way that when the button is pressed, it doesn't actually go down far enough.
2. **Monitor light:** Does the monitor's power light go from amber to green? If the monitor light remains amber, it could be that the monitor cable is loose. The unit is actually booting up just fine—you just cannot see it.
3. **BIOS:** You should see some text on the screen within a few seconds of powering up. If you don't, the BIOS chip could be corrupted. Most likely you will see the BIOS information, but look for messages that indicate some sort failure. Text like "No hard bootable drive found" can meaning anything from there being a floppy disk in the A drive to a dead hard drive. Search on the Internet for any message you get that you don't understand.

4. **Operating system:** Once the hardware has been checked out by the BIOS, it starts the operating system. Make sure there are no error messages at the start that might indicate a failure. If the operating system does not make it all the way to a fully operational desktop, try to determine what the last successful step in the process was. If you compare this with a working computer you may be able to figure out which step was the one the system choked on.

If your computer is officially dead in that it doesn't turn on, you can attempt to place the hard drive in another computer as the second drive. This may allow you to recover important files or to see if the drive can be used in another computer. For instance, you may have an old unit that is fine except that its hard drive died. Replace the dead drive with the working drive from the dead computer. If you can't access the files on your hard drive using another computer, you probably have to rebuild your system. Naturally, you may want a second opinion from a computer technician before taking this drastic step.

Rolling Back Your Data

Newer versions of Windows have a system called "system restore" that creates "restore points." If something has gone horribly wrong, this system restore can restore your computer to a previous state. If this technology is not part of your operating system, it can usually be added via third-party applications. The main downside is that these rollback systems require a great deal of hard disk space. If you have an older computer it may not have the necessary drive space.

Rollbacks are useful when the problem is a new application that mauled the system, but it is not a substitute for a backup system. If your hard drive dies, all the rollbacks will be gone.

Recovering Data

After you determine that your system has been compromised and before you proceed with any other recovery steps, you will want to attempt to recover crucial data if possible. Don't worry about recovering application files or system files, but if you have crucial data that is not in your last backup, you should try to save it to some removable media. These files might include word-processor documents, spreadsheets, and email folders. Even if the files have been corrupted or declared lost, some specialized utilities can often recover some or all of the data.

Rebuilding a System

If your system has been compromised by an attacker or by a virus that can't be cleaned, the generally accepted course of action is to rebuild your system from scratch. There is too much chance that critical system files have been replaced and are working on behalf of the attacker. For instance, it is not uncommon for attackers to replace critical system files with ones that steal the passwords you type or create open connections to your system that the attacker can use at some point in the future to regain control of your system.

For this reason, you need to perform a complete rebuilding of your system. If you're not sure what to do, turn off your computer and call for technical help. Remember to write down any error messages that may appear.

16

Email and IM

Email messaging is arguably the most important mechanism of personal communication after the telephone. There is every reason to think that email messaging will continue to grow in importance. Instant Messaging for students has the same relationship to email as email has to the telephone. Students find it difficult to understand why anyone would waste time sending an email when they could "just IM." Unfortunately, both technologies come with many technical and social shortcomings.

Email

Email originated during the early mainframe days. There were no concerns about users pretending to be someone else or requirements for files to be transferred. Email was not designed to operate in a global environment where executable files can be attached and sent with a click of a mouse button—yet another technology that did not yet exist. Email is the perfect example of a technology that people have tried to add security to after the fact. The results are not as good as they would have been had the system been created with security in mind. Few people use email-based security systems because those systems tend to be convoluted to operate and expensive to obtain.

The central problem with email is that it is easy for the sender to fake his or her identity. If you are suspicious of a message, confirm the message with the sender by telephone or by sending a separate email message asking for confirmation.

Careless email usage can result in a number of unintended consequences. For instance, an email message sent out to a very long list of recipients in the "To" field can result in all the recipients being provided a virtual address book—to which they may not be entitled. The simplest way to avoid this breach of confidentiality is to put all the email addresses for a mass email in the BCC (blind copy) address field in your email message. This will hide all the other email addresses. It also has the benefit of preventing a potential disaster in case a recipient accidentally clicks "reply to all" when he or she intended to reply to the sender. The last thing you need to have happen is to hit "reply to all" and write back to sender: "Great idea, but the rest of the morons here won't get it." After they get it, you'll get it.

Instant Messaging

Instant message may be one of the newer rages, but it also goes back to the early days of computer history. The first instant messaging was one person sending a line of text to another person on the system. Soon, instant messaging became a two-way conversation. As with email, the original versions of instant messaging did not envision file transfers, video, and telephone service. Unlike email messaging, there hasn't been an expectation that instant messaging systems work together. The instant messaging world is split between AOL, MSN, Google, and Yahoo!. There are IM clients who can interoperate with all the three systems, but one has to create accounts on each system to be accessed. Some IM systems deal with the interoperability issue by building their own separate networks. Many of the newer IM systems are actually very secure, but they have fewer members because of their newness. Small size isn't a problem if you want a solution for everyone in the school, but it becomes an issue when dealing with the public becomes important.

Instant messaging is so easy to install and to use that users rarely realize how dangerous it can be. Frequently the user is so confident there are no problems associated with using an instant messenger that he or she will not even mention that they have installed one on their computer. If only their lack of concern were justified. Viruses, thieves of private information, and remote operation of the victim's computer are just some of the risks. Instant messages are also liable to be intercepted because messages are transmitted over the Internet in plain text. And the world of email spam has spilled over in the IM world—where it's called *spim*.

There are a number of products that can secure IM communications. The key requirement is that all parties use the same security program. It is also important to make sure that everyone has the most recent version of the instant messaging software, because security holes are found and patched on a regular basis.

17

Disk Imaging

A disk-imaging system takes a snapshot of a hard drive to perfectly record the hard drive at a point in time. Technically, disk imaging is a form of backup, but when it is combined with a policy of purchasing uniform hardware it becomes a very efficient mechanism for installing, maintaining, and repairing computers. Uniformity is the friend of the harried technical support person and disk imaging is a key element to maintaining uniformity.

There is a fine distinction between a backup system, which records every file on a disk, and a disk-imaging system, which makes an exact copy of the disk. Backup systems don't record the formatting and partitioning of the disk drive. This means that to restore to another drive, the new drive needs to be formatted and partitioned before data can be transferred to it. This could take hours. Disk imaging also has an advantage in that it makes it copy when the disk is not being used. Disk imaging is done first by booting the computer off a special floppy disk or bootable CD-ROM so that none of the files on the drive to be imaged are in use. Backup systems work from within the computer's operating system. This is important because getting a perfect copy of a drive may not be possible if the system is in use. All of this assumes you want a perfect copy of your disk. In most cases, the traditional backup software is more than adequate and it is easier to operate—though recent versions of imaging software are easy to use.

Potential Uses of Disk Imaging

- **Rescue disk.** A disk image can restore a computer to a previous state. It's not a bad idea to make an image before making a major change to your computer. If things don't go well, you can go back to the original condition.
- **Resetting a computer.** Publicly used computers, such as those in a school computer lab, can use imaging systems to return to a base status. This process wipes out any virus or program that should not be there. Every day you have a fresh computer.
- **Computer upgrade.** Imaging makes it easy to upgrade large numbers of computers. You may be able to upgrade one computer, image it, and then share that new system with tens or hundreds of other computers. You can potentially save thousands of hours of work. In some cases you may be able to take a before-and-after set of images of a computer to be upgraded and distribute the differences between the two images. If the other computers use the same base image, the addition of the alterations,

some times called "deltas," should be just as effective as reimaging the entire drive.

- **Repair.** A disk image can be a fast way to fix a tricky computer program. Rather than spending hours troubleshooting some weird combination of ailments, you can restore the system to a known good condition. When restoring a computer only takes 10 or 20 minutes, it is difficult to justify spending hours to figure out an obscure problem.

Some Concerns with Using Disk Imaging

There are a few downsides to disk imaging which are important to consider. The first problem is that unless you are making frequent images, the image you have to restore from will not have all the latest user settings. Even if you force your users to put all their data on the network server, there are still many forms of data that will be stored on the user's computer. For example, the user's browser will keep lots of useful information on the local drive. Personalized screen savers and wallpaper images are stored locally. Programs such as Outlook may be storing email and calendar information on the local drive. Even settings in Word that tell the program to store documents on the network drive will go back to pointing at the "My Documents" directory on the local drive. In other words, a great deal of information is stored on the user's computer. Restore the unit to its original condition and you will learn how important those little details can be to the user.

A number of vendors have come along to save this multitude of personal settings. These "personality transfer" programs copy all these settings to a network drive or to a CD-ROM. After the unit is restored by a disk image, the settings are transferred back to the unit. If all goes as planned, the user will not see any difference between the old and new computer.

A potential problem with disk imaging is that it can make your network look as if it were full of illegal software. During the installation of an operating system, the installation process examines all of the hardware components on the computer being installed. The newly installed operating system uses this collected information to create a computer-specific identifier. If you use a disk image from one computer to install other computers, the software will notice that the hardware it is expecting to see is no longer there. It may assume that the software has been illegally installed. It has no way to know that you have a legal copy of the software sitting on the shelf. Assuming it's illegal, the software will cease functioning and/or report you to the software's maker. While some vendors offer solutions to this dilemma, a smaller operation may decide it's easier to install each unit and then make a separate image of that specific unit.

18

Recovering from a Disaster

The first thing you have to know about disasters is that they don't always look like a news story or an action film. Yes, a hurricane is a real source of concern if you live in certain areas of the country, but a disaster need not be dramatic—most are not. A disaster is anything that stops your ability to work. The building doesn't have to burn down to bring your computer operation to its knees. The power going out, for example, is more than enough. Perhaps asbestos has been found and your building has been sealed off with plastic sheets and duct tape. In this case they may not even allow you to get the backup tape or any of your equipment. Perhaps your equipment has to be sent to a decontamination lab and will not come back for 3 months. If your insurance does not cover purchasing new equipment under such conditions, you may end up wising that the units had burned up.

Disaster Plans

No matter what the size of your organization, you need some sort of plan describing what your organization should do if disaster strikes. This plan needs to be known to the administration in case you're on vacation when things go wrong. You may want to consider testing the plan to make sure people understand it and are capable of carrying it out.

One size does not fit all. The plan should handle a variety of scenarios. A plan that assumes the entire network staff perished in a fire that consumed the building and all of its equipment is not the right one when the water main bursts and you have to relocate to another building down the street. Your plan should be able to handle the following scenarios.

- Complete loss of everything;
- Equipment and materials are inaccessible for a short period of time;
- The building is unusable, but the equipment can be taken with you to another location;
- The system is compromised by hackers and/or virus attacks; and,
- Technical staff is unavailable.

While every organization will have a different view of what constitutes a disaster and the amount of money and effort it is willing to spend to remedy the situation, there are a few basic steps that all plans should include.

- Contact numbers for people who would need to be contacted during an emergency. This list should be in the hands of multiple people and it should include everyone's number—don't assume that you will have access to the rolodex sitting on your desk or that your Palm Pilot will be working.
- Have a list of computer vendors in the area.
- Have a list of computer rental companies. This can save a lot of trouble if you know you'll be getting your equipment back within a few months.
- Have a list of help lines for the major software vendors your organization uses.
- Keep serial numbers, passwords, and other sensitive information available. Naturally, you don't want to be giving out this information freely. You might place this information in a sealed envelop that will be kept in a fireproof safe.

19

Websites

It seems that everyone and their grandmother has a website. That's because it's easy to create a website. It's more difficult to create a good website. The web has great potential for those who understand its strengths and weaknesses. The key thing to remember is that a website is an opportunity to communicate and not the communication itself. Too often web designers are told to "put up a website because everyone has one." That's like saying, "Write a book because everyone else has written one." You have to have something to say that will be valuable to the audience you want to reach. And don't cop out with defining your audience as the "general public." Once you are able to define the audience and what is of value to it, it will be more apparent what the site needs to accomplish.

Web Advantages

The web can do many things well. By understanding the web as a medium, you'll be better able to recognize the tasks for which it is well suited. Below is a list of some of the web's primary advantages as a medium.

- **Modifiable.** When the information changes, so too can the website.
- **Inexpensive.** Websites can be very inexpensive. Even professionally designed sites tend to cost much less than the equivalent book or video.
- **Diverse formats.** Websites can include virtually any form of communication.
- **Interactive.** Websites, unlike most other media, can interact with the user and promote interactivity between users.
- **External resources.** A website can link to materials on other websites.
- **Ease of use.** A website tends to be a nonthreatening way to access information.
- **Integrated feedback.** A website can provide for user feedback. The web's ability to change quickly means that feedback can result in near-real-time improvement. Even when users don't leave a message, they do leave evidence of their activities in the web log. These log files can provide useful information regarding how your site is being used.
- **Access control.** A developer can control access to the entire site or to specific parts of a site based on the user's identity.
- **Customizable.** A website can dynamically create webpages based on personal preferences and updated content.

- **Multiple users.** Unlike a library book, a virtually unlimited number of users can access the website's content simultaneously.
- **Multiple creators.** Multiple people can maintain the site at the same time and from various geographical locations.
- **Time independent.** Users can use the site at any time of day or night. Unlike radio and television, the content can be used on demand.
- **Hyperlinks.** Hyperlinks allow content to be arranged and connected so as to allow the user to explore content in nonlinear ways. For example, a book generally requires a sequential reading, while a webpage can contain links that allow the reader to "drill down" for related sources of information.
- **Ease of promotion.** Making your site known is easy and inexpensive. Listing your site on the major search engines is usually enough for the public to learn of your site's existence. It doesn't hurt to have a Super Bowl ad, but it isn't required.
- **Data sharing.** Websites can contain data and programs that may be downloaded for use at another time.

Web Design

A website can be created without great sums of money and with low levels of skill, as long as expectations are correspondingly limited. There is no problem putting up a simple website if that's what your school requires. No one believes writing a book or producing a television show is easy or without significant costs, but for some odd reason, when text and video are going to be used to create a website, the costs and difficulty factors magically disappear. As with Open Source software, the perceived low cost makes bosses assume that everything should be correspondingly cheap.

It's very important that the people asking you to construct a website understand that the age-old sliding scale between cost and quality continues to operate in the Internet world. If they don't understand, every dime you get budgeted will be begrudged and anything that doesn't look like CNN.com will receive askance stares.

With expectation levels set correctly, you can now start the hard work. As with everything, you get what you pay for. Large sites today cost many millions of dollars to build and to maintain. The requirement for text and video editors doesn't go away when the web is used. In addition to their help, you'll need graphic designers, webmasters, and computer programmers.

The importance of identifying your site's audience and determining what they will find valuable cannot be overstressed. Too many sites are essentially vanity sites. They proclaim "I was born on . . . then I did XY and Z . . . and here's even more stuff about me. . . ." You might be able to corner someone at a party and force him or her to listen, but a visitor to your site can escape with a click of the back button. Beware of gushy welcome messages and highfalutin mission statements. Remember: it's all about them and not about you.

You need to recognize as you get started that websites invariably change and grow indefinitely. Unlike books and television shows, there is no point where you can declare the site done and go home. Creating a website is much like bringing home a baby alligator from a Florida vacation. At first it's a cute novelty. Later it becomes a bit of a bother now that it has taken over your bathtub. Eventually it will be chasing you around the house as its next meal. Websites are extremely easy to start and very difficult to end. Make sure the site's structure can expand without major redesign and that funding will be available in subsequent years.

Now that you've been warned, the good news is that a website can transform how your organization does its work. Imagine cutting in half all the routine calls your office staff gets because the information is now posted on the website. You may be able to offer services that were previously not feasible. The web also has the ability to operate around the clock. Think outside the box and build a site that provides real value to your targeted audience.

Understanding the Lingo

The web is so much in the public eye that you may feel uncomfortable asking questions because "everyone knows what it is." In reality, many web terms in the public domain are not well understood. Below is a short list of some web-related terms.

- **Accessibility:** This is the degree of ease that a disabled user can operate the site. There are federal laws mandating that websites meet accessibility standards. More information can be obtained from: http://www.w3.org/WAI/.
- **Dynamic and Static Websites:** A static webpage is one that has been constructed in its final form by the web designer and has no changes between its design and the user's visit to that page. A dynamic page, on the other hand, is dynamically built by creating a template into which information will be inserted from a database when requested by the visitor's browser. A dynamic page is very useful when either content is changing or the page is being personalized for each user. A website may have both static and dynamic pages.
- **Frames:** Frames is a method by which a webpage is split into two or more regions. Each region can act independently of the other.
- **GIF:** This image format is primarily used for text, line drawing, and other images that use block colors and sharp edges.
- **Graphics:** Obviously photos and drawing are graphics, but items like a title bar or background image are also graphics.
- **Heavy:** This is web slang for a webpage or website that is slow to download. Unlike with a television image, the amount and complexity of what is being displayed can affect the speed of the display. Generally, the file size of the webpage combined with the file sizes of associated graphics will determine the "weight" of the page. Test the page using different browsers and different speed connections. Too many designers use fast computers and high-speed Internet connections when designing a new site. They sometimes forget to check the average user's experience during the creation process.

- **HTML:** HTML stands for Hyper Text Markup Language. The important thing to know about HTML is that it is not a computer programming language like Basic or Java. It can be thought of as a text processor where you insert the codes that make text bold, italic, and so on. For example: This is <B>bold text.</B> would display as: This is **bold text**. In other words, don't let the fact that you're not a programmer stop you from working with HTML.

- **JPEG:** This is the image format primarily used for photographs and other images that have gradations in tone and color.

- **Meta Tags:** Every webpage can have a number of descriptions that provide various types of information about that page—for example, the name of the web designer and a brief blurb about the webpage's purpose. These tags can be useful for Internet search engines because they will use the meta tag descriptions for their description of the webpage on their search result page. Meta tags can also be used to indicate the kid-safe rating of the site.

- **PNG:** PNG is a set of graphic formats that are intended to replace JPEG and GIF. PNG has been fairly successful as a replacement for GIF and less so for JPEG. In terms of technical considerations, PNG is generally better than the older JPEG and GIF standards. If your site has to deal with users with very old browsers, don't use PNG graphics.

- **Proxy:** A proxy is anything that stands in for another thing. Proxy servers can work for both incoming and outgoing Internet traffic. A proxy for your web server accepts traffic for your actual website and transfers the content to the user. This is most often done for security reasons. Proxy servers can also be used by a school to intercept all the web requests going to the Internet. Use of such a proxy server allows the school to filter Internet traffic—or at least to record it—and it can also increase the performance of the Internet connection. This last feat is accomplished by the proxy server keeping a copy of the content that passes through. The next user gets the content from the proxy server rather than having to go to the Internet. When you have many students going to the same sites, the performance increase can be dramatic.

- **Robot file:** Internet search engines, such as Google and Yahoo!, use programs called "spiders" or "robots" to find content to index. You may not want to have some of your site indexed. Search engines have no interest in indexing materials you don't want indexed. For example, you may have a folder on your web server with old versions of your site. You can tell search engines which files and folders to avoid by creating a text file with the name of "robot.txt." Here is a website that describes how to write a robot file and where to place it in your web server's file structure: http://www.robotstxt.org/wc/norobots.html

- **Web hit:** A "hit" is the most misused Internet statistic term. It's common to hear people refer to the number of hits a website is getting as proof of its popularity. The problem with a hit is that it measures the number of items sent from your web server to all the users that visited your site. If you have 10,000 visitors and your page only has text on it, you get 10,000 hits. If you add a banner graphic and two photos, you'll get 40,000 hits because you now have four items being downloaded.

Generally, the most meaningful statistic for measuring popularity is "unique visitors." You then look at the statistics which measure how long the average visitor stayed on the site. This is sometimes referred to as the "stickiness" of the site. The first measure tells you that people are finding your site and the second tells you how interesting it was—though you need to be concerned that long visits are not due to the user being confused by your menu layout.

- **Webpage:** This is a single page of a website.
- **Web-safe colors:** A web-safe color—and there are a little over 200 of them—will not shift its color depending on the user's software and hardware. While the shifted color won't be vastly different, it may become different enough to ruin your design. For example, a rich, deep red on a Mac computer may appear blood red on a PC. Not a problem if the site is for the Red Cross.
- **Web server:** Beginners often assume that a website requires special software running on a dedicated web server to operate. While this is true for complicated websites, a web server can simply be a file directory on a computer that is accessible to the public. HTML pages do not require special software to be readable by web browsers.
- **Website:** A site is one or more webpages that make for a contiguous body of work. Because pages and the associated materials on them can exist in multiple locations on the Internet, a site is really what the site's creator declares it to be. Generally, it is limited to what they have control over.
- **XHTML:** This is the transition language between HTML and XML. It's basically a stricter form of HTML, but not as strict as pure XML. HTML allows the user to make lots of mistakes and survive. This is one of the reasons millions of people have been able to create a website after only a few hours of work. XHTML forces designers to follow the rules. If you've followed the HTML rules in the past, XHTML will be an easy transition.
- **XML:** XML stands for Extended Markup Language. This is a superset of HTML. It's still understandable to the nonprogrammer but has much more power.
- **URL:** This is a web address. There are some arguments over what "URL" means, but "Universal Resource Locater" is as good as any. The common misconception is that a URL is only the address of a website. All the links and external objects, such as graphics, have URLs.
- **Usability:** This is the art of making a website functional and easy to use. Placement of menus, text size, width of margins, and even the colors used can dramatically affect the usability of a website.

Building a Major Website

Building a major website often requires a development team with a variety of skills. The concept for the site is always the most important ingredient in a website's development, but it is doubly important when a group is working together. You cannot afford to have your workers working toward different goals. The result will be that none of the goals will be achieved.

The skills that you will need for a major website are as follows:

- **Project leader:** Develops the concept for the site, protects the vision for the site during the development process, and makes sure the group works well together.
- **Graphic designer:** Focuses on the appearance and layout of the site. They also create the images and graphics for the site. Often the graphic designer will help create templates for the website.
- **Programmer:** Responsible for web programming. Many of the advanced features in modern websites require some level of programming skill. The programmer may also handle the HTML coding.
- **Database administrator:** Handles the management of the databases. Frequently, a website is constructed to provide access to a currently existing database, such as student records. While the programmer might be able to handle the database integration, the database administrator usually wants to be involved so as assure that the data is not being compromised.
- **Editor:** Editing for the web is a specialized skill because the lack of screen space requires a terse writing style capable of being understood by a user skimming the text. The editor also has to be comfortable with web terminology and have a good feel for when text becomes too laden with jargon.
- **Content specialist:** Responsible for the accuracy and relevancy of the site's content.
- **Publicist:** If the site requires that the public know about it, a publicist can help get the word out. This may mean Internet-based advertisements or it could mean ads in traditional media. An Internet-savvy publicist will understand the do's and don'ts of Internet advertising and will know how to achieve high rankings on the major Internet search engines.
- **Attorney:** This person makes sure you don't get sued and that you secure the appropriate trademarks.

Web Security

Websites come with a number of security concerns. One of the first decisions for your school to make is the physical location of the web server. Small schools should consider using a commercial hosting firm or asking a larger school for help. Large schools may want to consider creating and hosting a web server on their own network. The decision to stay in-house or go to an external host is a complex one and one that cannot be decided simply based on the size of the organization. Factors like the cost of Internet bandwidth in your area and the cost and quality of technical support are all part of the equation.

The decision about who will host your website is not to be made lightly. While the information on a web server is usually public, a web server can become a security vulnerability through which other machines on your computer network may be compromised. It may seem safer to have your website in your physical control, but often such is not the case. Similarly, it may seem less expensive to host your own website, but this may not be true, either.

Web servers are popular targets for attack. Attackers are looking for personal information and other sensitive information. If your website links to sensitive information, such as personal records, caution is called for. Many of the most serious security breaches have been due to the failure to protect sensitive information stored in web-accessible databases. There are no simple solutions. You must constantly ask what forms of protection are being used to protect your data. If you don't get satisfactory answers, go elsewhere or avoid involving sensitive information.

Domain Names

Domain names are aliases for 16-digit IP numbers. The names have no function on the Internet other than to translate memorable names into meaningful numbers. Quick, how many telephone numbers do you know? You probably know your home, work, cell phone numbers, and perhaps the numbers of a few close friends. How many Internet websites can you write down? Equally as important, where would you find IBM or CNN on the web? A good domain name for your school will be easy to remember, unlikely to be mistyped or misspelled, quick to enter, and not easily confused with another school's name.

Figure 17. DNS Root Structure

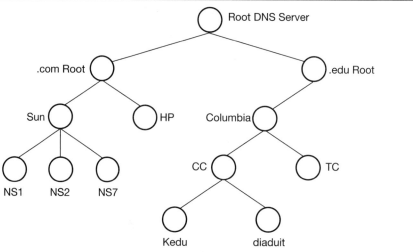

The DNS system finds the IP address associated with a domain name by doing a hierarchical search of DNS servers. To find kedu.cc.columbia.edu, the DNS system looks first for the .edu DNS server, then to Columbia DNS server, and so on until the authoritative DNS answers with the required IP address. This hierarchical system allows the Internet to encompass billions of addresses without creating a massive database at any single location.

The key thing to remember about domain names is that they need to be renewed. Renewal periods can range from one to 99 years. If you forget, the domain name may be taken over by another person and then used to extort money from you. So, once you commit to a domain name, be sure to renew it regularly so that your investment in that name is not forfeited. This warning is especially true if your school uses a name with the "org" domain structure, for example, school.org. Domains with the "edu" domain structure (i.e., school.edu) are safer because only schools can get them. You may ask why schools don't always have an "edu" domain name. The reason is because "edu" extensions are now reserved for universities. K-12 schools now use domain names like school.k12.ny.us. Some schools avoid the long domain names by using the "org" domain structure, initially designed for nonprofits and nongovernmental entities. By the way, a school can have multiple domain names. You just need to make sure having more names does not result in confusion.

20

Blogs and Wikis

Not everything on the web is a traditional website. Blogs and Wikis are two forms of websites that offer new and exciting ways to handle information. A blog is essentially an online journal. A wiki can be thought of as a website that can be edited by its users via their Internet browsers.

Blogs

Blogs are excellent for sites with frequently changing content that would fit into a journal-type of format. A blog would be wonderful for the school's activities and upcoming events. It could easily replace the school's weekly paper or sports flyer. It would not, however, be very suitable as a website representing the school to visitors, because blogs are not designed to present content that does not change—for example, directions to your school or the school's list of courses.

Blogs allow for interaction with the visitors via comment forms. After each posting in the blog, visitors may be allowed to post their own views. The views are listed below the article that is being commented on. This, of course, can have mixed results. Most blog servers allow for the owner of the blog to review comments before they are posted and all servers allow owners to delete unwelcome comments.

One of the most compelling features of a blog is a communications systems called RSS (Really Simple Syndication). RSS allows a visitor to a blog to subscribe to the site. The user's RSS reader, which may be incorporated in the Internet browser or operated as a separate program, periodically checks all of your RSS subscriptions, called *feeds*. The reader connects to your subscribed blogs and reports back the existence of new articles. The notice of new articles looks very much like a list of new email messages in an email client. When you click on the article notice, it opens to show a blurb of what is on the blog. If you are interested, you can click once again to be taken to the complete article.

RSS system greatly simplifies the process of checking for new content. One of the major problems with traditional websites has been a lack of a good way to announce changes. So your school may have changed the last day for early registration from the seventh to the sixth, but unless people visit your website, they won't know. RSS is a perfect solution for this type of problem. It allows users to track changes in way that is efficient and unobtrusive.

Wikis

Wiki is a term that comes from the Hawaiian phrase *wiki wiki*, meaning quick. Wikis live up to their name for quickness when it comes to changing content. Visitors to a wiki site can click on an "edit this page" button and change content on the spot. Wikipedia is the largest wiki site, with well over a million pages. All of its content has been created by visitors to Wikipedia. You can go there now and create or edit your own article. While one could argue that a wiki would probably be a disaster as a public school website, it could be fantastic as a mechanism for group writing for a language class.

Both blog and wiki servers can be found in commercial and open-source versions. It is worth your time to an install test server to get a feel for the technology. If you don't want to install a server just yet, you can use one of the many public free sites. There is no doubt that these new technologies will continue to grow as schools better understand their properties.

21

Fixing Problems

One of the key attributes of a good technologist is the ability to solve problems. The inherent complexity of combining multiple forms of computer hardware and software produces network environments that may never have been anticipated by any of the vendors involved. And, naturally, there is the ever-present issue that bugs of various types may be affecting the expected behavior of software or hardware. Fortunately, everyone else is in the same boat as you and there are methods for determining the source of even the most abstruse problems.

Identifying Problems

Identification is the first and most important step to solving a problem. It may also be the most difficult step. A user may report that his floppy drive no longer works. Sounds like a simple problem of a bad floppy drive. You bring a replacement unit only to find that it still does not read the user's disk. You then look closely at the disk to discover that the user was attempting to read a Mac floppy disk on a PC.

Below are some common steps to identifying a problem, using the "floppy disk drive" problem above as an example.

1. Get a report about what is really happening. You will often find that "my floppy drive does not work" really means it does not read a specific disk.
2. Ask users to write down any error messages they may see on the screen. Also ask if they hear unusual sounds.
3. Is the problem repeatable? Sometimes an otherwise healthy computer will have a temporary problem that can be resolved with a rebooting of the computer. Many problems will not return after a reboot. If that turns out to be the case, consider the problem to be over. If the problem is repeatable, you have a problem that should be solvable. Trying to figure out why a problem happened just one time is almost always a waste of your time.
4. If appropriate, have the user try the same action on another computer. This will tell you if the problem is specific or general. However, in the case of a floppy disk issue, you may want to consider the possibility of a virus. If that is a possibility, don't use the floppy disk in other computers until the disk has been scanned for viruses.

5. There are two main routes of problem solving from this point. The first method is to take the symptoms and error messages and enter them into an Internet search engine to see if a solution can be found. The second method is to use the time-honored process of elimination.

6. Contact any vendor that might be involved. If your floppy disk problem appears to be related to a known bug in the operating system, see if the manufacturer of the floppy disk drive or of the computer has a patch.

7. Before taking steps to fix a problem, assess the ramifications of data loss and service interruptions. Back up the data and consider waiting until after working hours to try corrective measures.

8. Record your efforts just in case the solution you found doesn't work. In fact, it's not uncommon for a solution to cause a problem worse than the problem being fixed. Repeat these steps until the problem is resolved. "Resolved" doesn't mean the source of the problem is fixed. At some point you may decide the problem is easier fixed by installing a new floppy disk drive.

Process of Elimination

The process of elimination for solving technical problems is a combination of flow chart of "if not this then that" boxes and a cost/risk analysis. One of the central ingredients of the process of elimination is the requirement that only one variable is changed at a time. Take the floppy disk drive problem, for example. Moving the floppy disk drive to another computer and trying a new disk doesn't identify the problem when the unit starts working. It could be the result of the move to the new unit or it could be the result of using a new floppy disk. It would have been better to have tried a different floppy disk or to have moved the floppy disk drive to another computer.

Over time you will learn that certain problems are more likely to occur than others. For instance, it's more likely that a diskette will have a problem than a floppy disk drive. It's more likely that the power cord is unplugged than that the computer power supply has died. In one office, the computer support person received a much higher than normal level of calls regarding dead computers on days when it rained. It soon became clear that the users were sliding their umbrellas and boots under the desk and pulling out the power cords in the process. These are the type of patterns that should be factored in.

Sometimes you shouldn't take the most obvious next step if that step is a risky one. Consider less dangerous alternatives first. It is up to you how many viable alternatives, even long shots, you should take before taking riskier steps.

Expense is akin to risk. You want to try less expensive solutions before considering more expensive solutions. Once again, you have to balance expense and the probability of success. One factor that is often forgotten is the cost of time. A less expensive solution that costs hours of staff time is no bargain. In the case of the floppy disk drive, you want to first try a few diskettes to confirm that you don't have a bad diskette. See if cleaning the floppy drive before replacing the drive helps. Drives on older units are prone to failure and the cost of replacements are so low that simply replacing the drive is more economical than would be extensive testing and diagnostics.

Replacing, rather than fixing, an old computer can also be cost-effective. The cost of computers has come down so much that replacing an old unit can be a viable alternative to fixing it. Let's assume that troubleshooting and repairing an older unit would cost $300 dollars and a new CPU would cost $600. It may appear that you have spent $300 too much. Yet the extra $300 not only makes the employee more productive because he or she has a faster unit, but the number of support calls will probably be less with new equipment. You should consider that the old unit would be scheduled for replacement in year even if it were fixed. So you are spending $300 on a unit that will be given away in a year's time. This math may not apply to every situation—especially in a budget-limited environment where monetary savings are consciously traded with staff time—but it is a decision-making matrix that you need to consider.

Log all support calls and the actions that are taken if multiple people are likely to be working on the same issues. Nothing screws up the process of elimination system as effectively as having multiple people working independently on the same problem.

Larger schools often use expensive issue-tracking programs to handle support calls. Smaller schools may find that using a notebook or sticking a few messages to the troubled unit's monitor may suffice.

Getting Technical Support

Not surprisingly, computer-oriented people like using computers to resolve computer problems. This was true in the old days of BBSes (computer bulletin board systems) and it is even more true with the advent of the Internet. The good news is that even the most obscure problem probably has volumes of information written about it; the bad news is, it can be difficult to determine which recommendations coming from those volumes can be trusted. Likewise, there are many support forums where technical questions can be asked, but the uninitiated user may not get a response because the experts are bored answering the same question for the millionth time.

In some situations you will not find anything that directly relates to your problem. This may be due to your not describing the problem in an understandable manner, or it could be that you have something new. Given the vastness of the Internet, it is more likely you have not described your problem correctly or have posted to the wrong subject group. If your problem is of a general nature, assume the first, and assume the latter if your problem involves odd combinations of hardware and software.

Asking a question that will be answered effectively requires care. First, make sure you have checked to make sure your question has not been asked and answered before. Questions that are repeats of previous messages are often ignored. Other people on the forum will not even bother to tell you that your question was just answered a few days back.

The key to getting help is to be as precise as possible with the description of the problem. Computer brand and model, the amount of memory, and other relevant information is usually a good place to start. Software versions are required for any problem relating to software. If you have error messages, list them first. If you have lots of details, put them after a summary of the problem. You don't want to overwhelm the reader. People on public forums are doing you a favor and shouldn't be expected to read volumes of details before getting to the central question.

Use online etiquette. This means being politic, clear, and to the point. Details, like replying to a message with "thanks" and copying the entire long message of the original, is considered poor form. The best way to know how to act is to read other postings to see how other users behave.

Better yet, if you have a major involvement with a specific item, join the related group before you have problems. Being a recognized community member is a real plus and you might read about a problem before it manifests on your system.

Many times your tricky problem will require a call to one of your vendors. There are a few important factors to remember when using telephone support.

- Use a speakerphone—you'll be on hold for a long time. Better yet, a wireless ear phone allows you to run to the next room.
- Get the names of the people you deal with and ask for any reference numbers to your situation—sometimes referred to as a "trouble ticket."
- If you are not satisfied with the response you're getting or feel the person is unable to answer your question, ask to be "escalated." Most support systems have two or three "tiers" of support. The upper-tier people are often required for the tricky problems. The first-tier folks are usually good enough for novice users.
- Let the support person know you are a professional technician (if you are). They'll take what you say more seriously. Of course, if that's not true, don't say it! They'll figure it out very quickly and doubly discount what you have to say.
- Keep records of what you've done up to that point and, if possible, sit in front of the unit that has the problem. The speakerphone comes in handy when you start entering commands on the keyboard.
- Deal with the right vendor. A video card might require a call to the computer vendor and/or to the vendor of the card. If your system is loaded with software, for example a Microsoft OS, the vendor of the computer and not of the software will provide support. Such software is labeled "OEM" (Original Equipment Manufacturer) and represents itself as coming from the OEM. In other words, you may tell everyone you have Microsoft Windows, but to Microsoft's support staff, you have XYZ's Windows. The minute you read the "OEM" part of your product's serial number, you'll be given the telephone number for the vendor.

Sometimes getting through on a vendor's free technical-support line is almost impossible. Vendors naturally want to encourage you to use their fee-based system for obtaining help. But before pulling out your wallet, you can try a few tricks. First, find out what part of the country the vendor's technical support is in. You can tell this by listening to the message saying their hours of operations are 6:00 a.m. to 6:00 p.m. Pacific Standard Time. If you're on the East Coast, call as early as you can so that you are not competing with the West Coast callers. Sometimes this works. The worst-case scenario is when you are an hour into the hold queue and the line is dropped—repeatedly. In these situations, call sales—they always pick up quickly—and ask to be transferred to the technical support for a "pre-sales technical question." That often gets you into a better queue because the technical people have to be readily accessible to the sales people.

Don't overlook using web forms and email messages for technical support. Simple questions can often get answered this way. It can make sense to send in a more complicated problem this way because it will get you an automatically generated reference number. Having a reference number may be able to get you placed into a shorter support queue because the system sees you as a return caller. It also gives the technician a written description of your problem when you finally get through. This will save a lot of time on the phone and the technician may be in a better mood because of that fact.

When you reach the point where you believe you have been unfairly treated, most large firms have special staff linked to the president's office. Complain to the president of the company and supply all the names, dates, and reference numbers that you can. If you have purchased a lot of items from them, let them know. If you are large enough to have a sales representative, let him or her know of your problems. Be firm but polite.

Volunteer Brigade

Schools and nonprofits don't have the money to hire big-dollar computer experts, but they do have something rich corporations don't have: goodwill. Many people are willing to volunteer for schools. The children of all these expensive computer experts have to go to school somewhere.

The volunteer pool does not have to be limited to the parents of children or even to people who know your school. There are many organizations that match volunteer computer experts with nonprofit organizations. The help these experts can provide can be invaluable.

Schools sometimes overlook the resources represented in their own student populations. Many high school students are technically savvy. With the appropriate supervision, they can be excellent resources for the high school and even for lower grades. These youth volunteers help you and they gain practical training with computers that can lead them to careers as computer technicians.

The key to using volunteer computer experts effectively is the appropriate matching of the task to the volunteer. Matching the volunteer's skills to the required tasks is important, but even more important is the issue of time requirements. If possible, volunteers should be given projects that do not have fixed deadlines. They have work lives that may not allow them to drop everything and come over to remove a virus or reboot a server. What they can do is take on projects, like designing a new network or upgrading computer memory over the weekend.

If volunteering is not a possibility, consider internships. Call up your local high school, university, or technical training school to see if they have students looking for internships. Like volunteers, assign them to projects with flexible time requirements. You also need to be aware that it's not fair to have an intern doing one simple job for the duration of the internship. Part of the deal is that they are exposed to a number of learning experiences. If it's done right, everyone wins. You might even find your next technical staff member through the internship process.

22

Remote Connections

As the speed, availability, and price of high-speed connections improve, the differences between your local network and the Internet decrease. At some point there will be no real difference between being on a local network and being connected via the Internet. That day is still a ways off, yet there are many compelling reasons to access your school's local network via the Internet. The two most common forms of remote connections are remote-control software and VPNs (Virtual Private Networks).

Remote Control Software

One way to "be at the office" while still being at home is to use a remote-control program. A remote-control program works by allowing you, working on one computer, to take control of another. The program sends your computer the screen display, keyboard strokes, and mouse movements of the computer being controlled. The illusion of remote control is that your unit at home has become the unit in the office.

There are a number of compelling reasons why remotely controlling another computer can be attractive. Some of these advantages are specific to working from home, while some are valid even if the computer being controlled is only a few feet away. Here are a few compelling reasons to use remote-control software.

- Accessing files and information located on your local computer when you are someplace else.
- Remotely monitoring another user's computer when he or she is experiencing a technical problem.
- Remote training can be accomplished by performing a task on the remote computer while the user who is being trained watches. You can also monitor what steps they are taking. Remote-control software can be set up for you to take total control over the remote computer—even if the remote computer's keyboard does not function—or both you and the local user may share control.
- Controlling a unit that is inside your network from home allows you to assess the health and performance of the network from a remote location.
- Some security systems, such as firewalls, allow connections from within a network but not from outside. Remotely controlling a computer on the network when you are actually outside the network can allow you to perform functions that would otherwise not be possible.

- A remote user can use programs on the remote computer that are not on the local computer. For example, a home user with an iMac can control a Windows- or Linux-based computer that might be in the office.
- Remotely controlling another unit allows you to perform work on another unit without tying up your main computer. For example, you can run a taxing program on a remote computer while you continue to work on your home computer. It's like doubling the power of your computer.
- Remote control has the perception of making "working from home" look like real work. For people who exclusively use the computer and the phone, there is not much difference between working from home via remote-control software and being physically at the keyboard.

VPNs

VPN stands for "Virtual Private Network." (See Figure 12 on p. 39.) It's a strange-sounding term unless you know the history of telecommunication lines. In the past—and to some extent today—businesses wanting connections between different locations purchased private telecommunication lines from the telephone company. These private lines were called "private" because these lines were not shared with other customers. Privacy came at a very high cost. These lines were unaffordable to anyone other than the richest customers.

The Internet has made it convenient for an organization to connect all of its locations, but its public nature brings with it the problem of security. Internet communications are potentially open to numerous people. A bank, for example, does not want even the slightest chance that its account numbers and passwords could be seen by any unauthorized party. The consequences of a breach would make private lines look cheap by comparison.

The solution for obtaining the security of a private network while keeping the price advantages of the Internet is the VPN. A VPN creates connections that are virtually private due to their use of encryption. Encryption makes the content being transmitted between any two VPN points unreadable to anyone on the public network. It is important to note that a virtually private network on the Internet does not share a true private line's advantage of guaranteed bandwidth. When the telephone company supplied a private line, it was dedicated to just that customer's use. Traffic from other customers could not affect performance because they were on different physical lines. Internet traffic may affect the "private" traffic because all the traffic competes for the same bandwidth.

A VPN can be used in some of the ways in which a remote-control program is used. Home workers often use VPNs for connecting to the office. The difference between VPN technology and remote-control software is that a VPN does not require a host computer on the local network. The VPN works by extending the network to the home computer. The home worker's computer becomes an integral part of the local network. Remote-control software, however, only makes the home unit appear to be on the local network because of it taking over a unit that is on the local network.

These differences may appear subtle, but they are quite important. For example, if you have a remote office with dozens of computers, it does not make sense to have each remote worker controlling a unit on the network. VPNs are especially good for situations where physically separated networks of computers need to be integrated via the Internet. For example, the main office has an employee database with sensitive information. A VPN would allow another office to access this database as if they were on the local network. By comparison, using remote-control software would require a number of computers to be sitting idle in the office with the database.

Security Issues

When you make another computer part of your network, all the security standards applied locally need to be applied to the new addition. Often, the remote computer is a staff member's home computer and the responsibility for its security may be a gray area. This gray area can result in the remote computer having full access to the local network without the benefit of the network's security precautions. These remote units will most likely become the weakest links in your security system.

Passwords and Callback

The more sensitive the information being accessed, the better the password needs to be. A VPN connection must have a very good password associated with it, given the damage that could result from a breach. Look at the section on creating strong passwords and consider creating a separate password for the VPN login.

Some remote systems use telephone dial-up connections. In some ways this is safer than an Internet connection because the information is not traveling over the Internet. Hackers use automated dialing units, called "war dialers," to run through all the telephone lines belonging to an organization. These war dialers seek modems that can be called up at a later time by the hacker. If your school is using modems for dial-in access, consider using a "callback" security method. Callback works by cutting the connection after the user name and password have been entered. The unit being called then calls back the telephone number for the user who just logged in. If a hacker had been able to break in, the unit will still call to the legitimate user. The hacker is presumably not physically in the user's home.

Possible Privacy Issues with Remote Control

The most common uses of remote control within a school are technical support and training. When a user calls with a mysterious computer ailment, the next best thing to visiting the user is to use remote control to see what is happening. In some cases, the remote user can demonstrate to the user the proper way to carry out the desired task.

Users will naturally wonder if they might be observed at other times. Most remote-control systems have an option of letting the user know when the remote agent is watching. This warning can be deactivated by the administrator. One may wonder why this is an option. Sometimes an organization has a valid reason for observing a user surreptitiously—for example, when someone is suspected of committing a criminal act with the computer.

Although surveillance is legal, and sometimes required by law, it is important to let the staff know that monitoring is possible. These topics should be well defined in the organization's policy manual. Staff can understand that this policy is an unfortunate requirement of our modern society; however, they will not accept your school keeping this policy secret.

23

Foundations of the Internet

The Internet is perhaps the most surprising development in an age defined by constant surprise. Whether you believe the Internet is the most wonderful development ever or a conglomerate of the world's basest elements, it has to be understood.

Internet Structure

The first question many newcomers to the Internet ask is the location of its headquarters. The answer: nowhere and everywhere. The home user with a modem is just as much a part of the Internet as any of the major ISPs (Internet Service Providers). Being part of the Internet requires following Internet standards. The vast collection of computers, connection types, and communication services that comprise the Internet only work together because there is an agreed set of standards that allows them to interoperate.

"Ah ha!" you may be saying. Who creates these standards? The answer, once again, is everyone and no one. Groups of volunteers gather in an open forum to discuss new standards. The standards group puts out an RFP (Request for Proposal) and anyone can submit their solution to the standards body. The public can also comment on the various proposals. The standards group has significant incentive to listen to public opinion because an unpopular standard frequently does not get implemented. Over time, the major computer companies have become heavily involved in many of the standards bodies. Yet they still have to come up with a solution that the public and their customers will find acceptable.

History of the Internet

The Internet began in the late 1960s as a U.S. government–funded network for university and commercial research.[12] The Internet later became the responsibility of the NSF (National Science Foundation). The NSF maintained the Internet as an academic-orientated network. As the Internet's financial potential became obvious, private enterprise wanted to participate for commercial reasons. Because of the

---

12. A Brief History of the Internet, by B. M. Leiner, V. G. Cerf, D. D. Clark, R. E. Kahn, L. Kleinrock, D. C. Lynch, J. Postel, L. G. Roberts, & S. Wolff, Internet Society, December 10, 2003. Available at http://www.isoc.org/internet/history/brief.shtml#Origins

NSF's government-based funding, commercial use was forbidden. Eventually, the NSF stepped aside to allow commercial entities—primarily the major telephone companies—to run the main backbones. Today's Internet is a continuation of that private system. Yet the standards-based approach has continued.

One of the most important aspects of Internet history is the culture that has grown around it. The fact that the Internet started off as a U.S. academic network has given it a culture that it would not have had had it originated from a commercial or military network. The main embodiment of this culture can be found under the term *netiquette*. Netiquette is the do's and don'ts for user behavior. For example, typing in ALL CAPS is considered the equivalent of yelling. Individuals who type every message in all caps are considered dogmatic, thoughtless, or inexperienced. Multiple infractions used to get offenders ostracized or removed from the Internet. As the Internet grew, infractions began to be seen more as bad manners than as reasons for removal. Even so, it's important to understand these informal rules. Following netiquette is still important because it improves the effectiveness of your communication.

One of the most interesting aspects of the Internet has been its history of breaking down walls. Repressive governments—even nonrepressive governments—have tried to resist or to control the Internet. The Internet is an uncontrollable communication mechanism. Yet the Internet's educational and commercial benefits make it very difficult to exclude. No matter how angry a government might get, they recognize that cutting off access to the Internet would be disastrous for their business and educational communities.

A hallmark of the Internet seems to be its ability to take over a function and then revolutionize it in an unanticipated way. Some of the changes will be good and some will be bad. It is vital that your school understands that connecting to the Internet is a dynamic commitment that will require constant readjustment. It is also important that your students get an appreciation of the Internet as a societal force of nature carving through society's age-old structures akin to a wild river carving out bedrock.

Internet Standards to Know

Internet standards make the Internet what it is. It's important to be familiar with the more common terms because the standards they represent are frequently being used in almost every form of technology that communicates.

- **TCP/IP:** These are two related standards that describe how information is sent over the Internet.
- **DNS:** The Domain Name System translates domain name, such as www.whitehouse.gov, into a numerical address, 63.211.66.91. (See Figure 17 on p. 106.)
- **FTP:** Specifies how files can be transferred over the Internet. Many people now use a secure form of FTP called SFTP. SFTP standards for "secure FTP."
- **Telnet:** This system allows users to log in to a remote computer. As with FTP, its security is considered weak.

- **IMAP:** This is one of the two major email storage standards. The other is POP. IMAP is frequently used by organizations because it allows the user to store email folders on a central email server. This allows the user to access his or her email folders from any location.
- **POP:** This is the most common email system on the Internet. Anytime a user gets an email account from an ISP, it is likely to be a POP email account. POP stores mail in an in-box and the user downloads the email to his or her system. Once on the local system the email system can store the message in a local folder. ISPs tend not to offer IMAP because it would require them to provide huge amounts of storage space for all the email folders. POP is less functional, but less expensive to operate.
- **SMTP:** This standard describes how email servers will communicate with one another. This is how email makes it from place to place.
- **HTML:** A markup language that allows Internet browsers to display a webpage.

24

Working with People

Technologists often act as if they are only responsible for taking care of the computers. They miss the fact that it's the users of the computers that really count. Users are sometimes even treated as uninvited guests. No matter how good you are with technology, it won't matter if you're bad with people.

Managing Change

Managing change is the key to working with technology. Technology rarely stands still and people's expectations of what technology should do constantly changes as well. The problem is that any organization with more than one person will have divergent expectations.

Schools share common grouping types. Your first step is to assess the type of groups in your school. Below are some of the groups that are almost always found in any organization.

- **Leaders.** These are the bosses. They need to be paid attention to because they are probably going to be approving your budget. You need to sell them on your plan. They may not understand the technology but they will be paying close attention to general opinion among the staff.
- **Opinion leaders.** These people are the most respected people. Their power is based on their personality and connections more than it is on their job position. Other people will tend to follow the opinion leader's views. If your plan runs afoul of them, don't expect support from the rest of the school.
- **Power users.** These people push their software and hardware to the limits. They usually have a good understanding of technology. They are probably in the opinion leader role as well. If the power users have a different view from your plan, their views will be taken as facts that could be used to counter your facts. Unfortunately, the power users may be great at operating their favorite software application while quite ignorant of computer technology in general. You have to educate them because the rest of the school may not know their limitations. They are just the person "who knows all that tech stuff."
- **Active resisters.** Some people don't like change under any circumstances. Perhaps they are a few years from retirement and the last thing they want is to have their life turned upside down. Often they are in a position to protest with impunity. You may win them over to your camp,

but consider yourself lucky if you can negotiate a deal with them that lets them change as little as possible in return for their support.

- **Passive resisters.** These people will stay silent but have no intention of helping the process. You have to figure out who they are.
- **Supporters.** Sometimes supporters can be more than they seem. The person most in favor of your plan may be intending to co-op the plan or has a different understanding of the project than what you have presented. Their requests can be tricky to handle because they will sound reasonable. This is when it's a good thing to have support from the organization's leaders. Someone has to come in to say that the new feature is great but not possible within the budget provided. Don't take your plan's supporters for granted.
- **Competitors.** Sometimes there are multiple plans for the same project. Hopefully you can work with anyone who has a meaningful plan. Multiple plans tend to result in none of them being approved. If you end up deadlocked, ask for some sort of objective review or test to settle the issue.
- **Risk takers.** Some people are willing to take the first step. These people are often willing to test the new system before it's rolled out to the entire organization. These people should be cultivated and appreciated.

You may not have all of these groups and you may have group types not described above. The key thing to remember is that there are groups, cultures, and informal networks that are just as important as anything found in the school's official tome of rules and regulations.

Vendors

As with all businesses, there are good and bad computer vendors. Check references, sign a contract, and make sure that your final payment is not due until the satisfactory conclusion of the job.

There are a few characteristics of computer vendors of which you need to be aware. The first is that vendors usually focus on a limited set of possible solutions. If you ask a vendor to come in to evaluate your school's situation, don't be surprised that the solution just happens to require the products for which they are authorized dealers. Computer salespeople often have a near-religious conviction when it comes to certain products. If you want to use an IBM PC and your vendor is an Apple vendor, don't expect to hear good things about the PC, and vice versa.

You need to know the built-in bias of the vendors with whom you meet. You may want to bring in a number of vendors if you're not sure about the general direction in which you want to go. So, if you are not decided between Windows, OS X, and Linux, you'll need to talk to vendors that represent each point of view. You cannot assume that any single vendor will give you an unbiased assessment of all three systems.

Many of the same rules apply to consultants. They are vendors of intellectual capital. They can be extremely useful in pointing you in the right direction. Yet you have to be careful to make sure the consultant does not have ties to vendors.

Otherwise, you may find yourself paying top dollar from a vendor who knows you're a sure thing. Good consultants will usually make it clear that they don't sell or represent people who sell equipment.

Consultants can also be used to set up new systems, to undertake custom programming, and to handle emergency support needs. If used correctly, consultants can add a lot of value. Unfortunately, clients seem to forget that consultants make their money by the hour. Consultants have a vested interest in staying on your payroll as long as possible. While a few shady consultants will drag out a job, most will simply ask you if you want additional services. Before you know it, you could double or triple your budget.

Contracts should make it clear what will be delivered, at what times, and by whom. You certainly don't want to pay everything until the contract has been completed. You may even want to put in bonuses if the work gets completed ahead of schedule. Consultants, especially programmers, seem to have a habit of completing 80% of their work and then losing interest in the remaining 20%. Sometimes this is because the last 20% is detail work and documentation, which is boring and tedious for them to do. You should always require documentation. Without it, it will be difficult for others to work on your system. Sometimes a consultant will seem dis-tant because she or he has run over the time planned for your job and is attempting to start work for their next customer. If you are not withholding a fair amount of money and a signed contract, don't be surprised if he or she simply disappears.

The Customer Is Always Right

We know that the customer isn't always right, but they should be treated as if they are. Your users are your customers. They may not be able to take their business elsewhere, but their unhappiness can poison your environment to the point that you wish you could go somewhere else. The key to user happiness is their feeling that they have been heard and appreciated. They'll understand that a limited budget comes with sacrifices and hardships if the options are explained clearly.

Frequently, the problem with users and their high expectations is that they do not understand the ramifications of what they are asking for. For example, it may appear easy to buy a scanner so that all the paper cluttering their desks can be eliminated. They know from purchasing home scanners that scanners are inexpensive. It seems like an obvious solution. Explain to them that the scanning might be easy to start but that saving images of all those papers will burden the file server, slow down the network, and could result in them not being able to find their papers. Remember, a scanned image is just a picture. If you don't remember that file0023.jpg is your class roster, you'll not be able to find it easily. When these details are explained, users will frequently change their minds and you've just saved yourself years of problems.

Talking to users is crucial for projecting future needs. Once again, what they say they want may not be what they really need. This is where merging your knowledge of technological trends, examples of similar organizations, and the history of your organization comes into play. One of the advantages of working on a low budget is that many of the possible future directions have already been taken by wealthier organizations. You can learn from their examples and determine which models most closely approximate your school's future needs now that prices have gone down.

Involve the users whenever possible. If another school is doing something similar to what you want to do, take a select group on a visit. Likewise, if the users are dead set on something that you don't think will work, take them on a visit to an organization that is similar to what they are asking for. Nothing is as powerful as hearing a third party describing their situation. If you do your fact-finding correctly, the users will perceive you as servicing them and not as their opponent. If your discussions degrade into a power play of who's right, you lose. You may prove your point in the end, but their pride will not allow them to say so. When something goes wrong with your new system, they'll be saying "I told you so."

If you cannot change the minds of the users, consider taking their path even if you believe they are wrong. Naturally, this advice does not apply if their path is illegal or prohibitively expensive. If you support them when you believe they are wrong, you'll find that they will be more willing to support you the next time. It also makes it far easier to the organization to admit a mistake has been made if no loss of face is involved. It's better for everyone to be wrong in the same boat than half be in the boat and the other half floating in the icy ocean.

Public Assistance

Don't underestimate the power of goodwill. It's easy to forget that the motivations that led you to give up fame and fortune to work in a school compel others, as well. Goodwill and an organization's budget seem to be inversely related.

Public assistance can take many forms, ranging from federal grants to donated equipment from the local community. There are many resources online about how to get help. An amazing number of rich people have died and left very specific grants. So even if your school has had little luck with general grants, don't be surprised if there is some niche grant that you can win.

Don't overlook local politicians. They usually have staff dedicated to community services. Working with local politicians can also be useful if they are involved in setting your organization's budget. It's difficult to cut the budget of an organization to which you just presented an outstanding community service award.

Remember that not all help is helpful. Grants can distort your goals and alter your systems in such ways as to produce more harm than good. It is common to find that grants are good at supplying the initial hardware and software but often lack money for the associated training and technical support. Donations from the local community can be fraught with peril. Before you know it, you have a hodge-podge of equipment and systems that are virtually impossible to coordinate and support.

Donated old computers rarely come with their original software—or with illegal copies of software. Yet if you refuse to accept donations, you may find that the community gets the impression that you don't need any form of help. One way to avoid this dilemma is to circulate a list of specifications for donated equipment so that you don't find yourself in the embarrassing situation of turning away useless computers.

25

Maintaining Your Own Sanity

We sometimes don't take care of the most important part of the network: ourselves. It's very easy to sacrifice ourselves for the perceived interest of the school. Running yourself into the ground is much like trying to save money with your car by not changing the oil. You can do it, but the long-term costs are severe.

Over-Commitment

One of the main sources of grief for a technologist in the school environment comes from over-commitment. This may be in the form of working too many hours or taking on responsibilities for which no training has been provided. Often this happens as a form of "mission creep." This is where a good job description can come in handy. While the higher-ups may not respect the agreement, it can at least bring rationality to a discussion of job expectations.

Keeping job requirements reasonable is also important for those who follow. While teachers have been teaching in schools for centuries, the school's technologist may be the first one the school has ever seen. The first person to hold that job has the potential to create a mistaken set of the job's requirements. When the next person assumes the job, they will have been set up for failure from the very start because what they do is not in line with the expectations.

Head off problems as early as you can. Crisis situations may get your boss's attention, but it is often difficult to implement a change during a crisis. Just as you should be monitoring the amount of free space on the file server so that new space can be planned for, make sure you're ready for new functions and systems before you're up to your neck.

Setting Expectations

Set reasonable expectations. Your staff doesn't necessarily know what a task requires. Educate them about the work you do. People have more of a problem with an expectation not being met than they do with the actual delivery date. Make sure you set expectations that you can meet. If you create a pattern of not meeting target dates, you encourage your staff to constantly check on your progress. This constant checking will annoy both everyone and will slow the work. If you're not meeting your targets, figure out why and change the parameters. Many times it will be a result of incorrect expectation-setting.

Expectations are not so much missed as misunderstood. Your boss may ask you to add a new printer to the network. The boss may have installed a printer at home, and it took him or her only a few minutes. It may take hours to install the same printer on the school's network, however. Unfortunately, your boss may never make you aware that you've failed to meet the expectation. You'll just go into his books as "slow," "lazy," or "not as good as a real professional." Perceptions accumulate over time.

If it's too late to set the expectation, report on what you do. The expectation that you're trying to live up to may have been set by the person formally in your position. They probably burned out and left you holding the bag of unrealistic expectations. The best you can do is to list what you actually do and hope they realize what happened to the last person and that their expectations for your job need to be readjusted.

Setting Priorities

It's rare that you can accomplish all the possible activities related to your job as quickly as you would like. You need to prioritize your work so that the truly vital tasks are completed. Less vital tasks might be done more efficiently at other times—for example, updating computers with security patches. If you can get free access to all the computers during lunch or at some other time when the users are away, you can have all the computers installing away at the same time. This is faster than standing over the shoulder of each user, tapping your foot. To make this task even faster, you might be able to download the required patch and burn it to a CD-ROM or put it on the network server. Your updating process will now fly because the patches are being loaded locally rather than over the Internet.

What should be considered priority tasks will depend on the environment. No mater what, having an effective backup is always at the top of the list. Your organization may not ask for it, but when their data disappears they won't understand why you don't have it. Antivirus protection and maintenance of the firewall also has to be given priority status. After that, it's up to you.

Survive and Prosper

Organizations have personalities, bosses have personalities, and you have a personality. If the personalities don't match up, consider finding another place of employment. It's reasonable to expect being able to change user expectations, but changing the culture of an organization isn't in the cards. Many times technical people obtain their current positions through a series of incremental steps. It's not uncommon for a computer-savvy teacher to be assigned to helping with the school's computer needs part time. At some point part-time help becomes a full-time job. There is no shame in realizing that computers aren't what you signed up for. If you cannot return to teaching full time, consider another school.

Sometimes you have to take a job with another school to have a chance at advancement. When your current job is based on a gradual series of advancements, those around you may not recognize that your role has changed. Rather than being the Technical Coordinator, you are, in their minds, still the math teacher who knows something about computers. Taking a job with a new school allows you readjust perceptions and work expectations.

Don't let a bad situation linger. If a situation is irredeemable, leave sooner rather than later. Staying on wears you down and makes it more likely that your performance reviews and references will suffer.

Remember Who You Are

Manage yourself with the same level of attention you give your computer network. The Peter Principal says that people are often promoted to level of their incompetence. In a way this makes sense. People keep getting promotions based on the good work they have done in past positions. Promotions stop when the work deteriorates. In poor organizations, the lack of training opportunities makes it all too possible that someone will be thrown into a position for which they are not suited—and there will be no training to rectify this situation. This is a serious problem for both the school and the floundering employee.

Another common problem is that the aspect of the job that made the job fun is no longer a feature of the new job. You may be great at the job but your enjoyment of your job is gone. Enjoyment should not be underrated. A good technologist constantly reads the computer magazines and practices with new systems. It's difficult to keep up with technical trends if enjoyment does not lighten the load.

This is not to say that promotions aren't good. Many people enjoy the higher pay and recognition. Being able to implement ideas that were previously beyond their purview is another good reason to climb the organizational ladder. But most people join a school for a specific reason. Remembering who you are and why you're working where you are is crucial to making the right job decisions.

Index

About the Author

Thane B. Terrill is Adjunct Associate Professor of computing and education at Teachers College, Columbia University and Director of Information Services at the Bahá'í International Community's United Nations Office, an international NGO (Non-Governmental Organization) with offices in New York City and Geneva.

Dr. Terrill has over 20 years experience teaching at a variety of grade levels in both public and private schools in the Boston region. Over the last dozen years, he has undertaken consulting projects both in the U.S. and internationally in the field of educational technology. He especially enjoys working on projects that solve challenging problems without access to big budgets.

Dr. Terrill will be running a blog related to the topics in this book at: **http://techshoestring.blogspot.com/**. Please stop by and share your experiences.